Programming Neural Networks
with Encog3 in Java

Programming Neural Networks with Encog3 in Java

Jeff Heaton

Heaton Research, Inc.
St. Louis, MO, USA

Publisher: Heaton Research, Inc
Programming Neural Networks with Encog 3 in Java
First Printing
October, 2011
Author: Jeff Heaton
Editor: WordsRU.com
Cover Art: Carrie Spear
ISBN's for all Editions:
978-1-60439-021-6, Softcover
978-1-60439-022-3, PDF
978-1-60439-023-0, LIT
978-1-60439-024-7, Nook
978-1-60439-025-4, Kindle

TRADEMARKS: Heaton Research has attempted throughout this book to distinguish proprietary trademarks from descriptive terms by following the capitalization style used by the manufacturer.

The author and publisher have made their best efforts to prepare this book, so the content is based upon the final release of software whenever possible. Portions of the manuscript may be based upon pre-release versions supplied by software manufacturer(s). The author and the publisher make no representation or warranties of any kind with regard to the completeness or accuracy of the contents herein and accept no liability of any kind including but not limited to performance, merchantability, fitness for any particular purpose, or any losses or damages of any kind caused or alleged to be caused directly or indirectly from this book.

SOFTWARE LICENSE AGREEMENT: TERMS AND CONDITIONS

SOFTWARE SUPPORT

Components of the supplemental Software and any offers associated with them may be supported by the specific Owner(s) of that material but they are not supported by Heaton Research, Inc.. Information regarding any available support may be obtained from the Owner(s) using the information provided in the appropriate README files or listed elsewhere on the media.

Should the manufacturer(s) or other Owner(s) cease to offer support or decline to honor any offer, Heaton Research, Inc. bears no responsibility. This notice concerning support for the Software is provided for your information only. Heaton Research, Inc. is not the agent or principal of the Owner(s), and Heaton Research, Inc. is in no way responsible for providing any support for the Software, nor is it liable or responsible for any support provided, or not provided, by the Owner(s).

WARRANTY

Heaton Research, Inc. warrants the enclosed media to be free of physical defects for a period of ninety (90) days after purchase. The Software is not available from Heaton Research, Inc. in any other form or media than that enclosed herein or posted to www.heatonresearch.com. If you discover a defect in the media during this warranty period, you may obtain a replacement of identical format at no charge by sending the defective media, postage prepaid, with proof of purchase to:

Heaton Research, Inc.
Customer Support Department
1734 Clarkson Rd #107
Chesterfield, MO 63017-4976
Web: www.heatonresearch.com
E-Mail: support@heatonresearch.com

DISCLAIMER

Heaton Research, Inc. makes no warranty or representation, either expressed or implied, with respect to the Software or its contents, quality, performance, merchantability, or fitness for a particular purpose. In no event will

Heaton Research, Inc., its distributors, or dealers be liable to you or any other party for direct, indirect, special, incidental, consequential, or other damages arising out of the use of or inability to use the Software or its contents even if advised of the possibility of such damage. In the event that the Software includes an online update feature, Heaton Research, Inc. further disclaims any obligation to provide this feature for any specific duration other than the initial posting.

The exclusion of implied warranties is not permitted by some states. Therefore, the above exclusion may not apply to you. This warranty provides you with specific legal rights; there may be other rights that you may have that vary from state to state. The pricing of the book with the Software by Heaton Research, Inc. reflects the allocation of risk and limitations on liability contained in this agreement of Terms and Conditions.

SHAREWARE DISTRIBUTION

This Software may use various programs and libraries that are distributed as shareware. Copyright laws apply to both shareware and ordinary commercial software, and the copyright Owner(s) retains all rights. If you try a shareware program and continue using it, you are expected to register it. Individual programs differ on details of trial periods, registration, and payment. Please observe the requirements stated in appropriate files.

This book is dedicated to my wonderful wife, Tracy and our two cockatiels Cricket and Wynton.

Contents

CONTENTS

Introduction

Encog is a machine learning framework for Java and .NET. Initially, Encog was created to support only neural networks. Later versions of Encog expanded more into general machine learning. However, this book will focus primarily on neural networks. Many of the techniques learned in this book can be applied to other machine learning techniques. Subsequent books will focus on some of these areas of Encog programming.

This book is published in conjunction with the Encog 3.0 release and should stay very compatible with later versions of Encog 3. Future versions in the 3.x series will attempt to add functionality with minimal disruption to existing code.

0.1 The History of Encog

The first version of Encog, version 0.5, was released on July 10, 2008. Encog's original foundations include some code used in the first edition of "Introduction to Neural Networks with Java," published in 2005. Its second edition featured a completely redesigned neural network engine, which became Encog version 0.5. Encog versions 1.0 through 2.0 greatly enhanced the neural network code well beyond what can be covered in an introduction book. Encog version 3.0 added more formal support for machine learning methods beyond just neural networks.

This book will provide a comprehensive instruction on how to use neural networks with Encog. For the intricacies of actually implementing neural networks, reference "Introduction to Neural Networks with Java" and "Introduction to Neural Networks with C#." These books explore how to implement basic neural networks and now to create the internals of a neural network.

These two books can be read in sequence as new concepts are introduced with very little repetition. These books are not a prerequisite to each other. This book will equip you to start with Encog if you have a basic understanding Java programming language. Particularly, you should be familiar with the following:

- Java Generics

- Collections

- Object Oriented Programming

Before we begin examining how to use Encog, let's first identify the problems Encog adept at solving. Neural networks are a programming technique. They are not a silver bullet solution for every programming problem, yet offer viable solutions to certain programming problems. Of course, there are other problems for which neural networks are a poor fit.

0.2   Introduction to Neural Networks

This book will define a neural network and how it is used. Most people, even non-programmers, have heard of neural networks. There are many science fiction overtones associated with neural networks. And, like many things, sci-fi writers have created a vast, but somewhat inaccurate, public idea of what a neural network is.

Most laypeople think of neural networks as a sort of "artificial brain" that power robots or carry on intelligent conversations with human beings. This notion is a closer definition of Artificial Intelligence (AI) than neural networks. AI seeks to create truly intelligent machines. I am not going to waste several paragraphs explaining what true, human intelligence is, compared to the current state of computers. Anyone who has spent any time with both human beings and computers knows the difference. Current computers are not intelligent.

Neural networks are one small part of AI. Neural networks, at least as they currently exist, carry out very small, specific tasks. Computer-based neural networks are not general purpose computation devices like the human brain. It is possible that the perception of neural networks is skewed, as the brain itself is a network of neurons, or a neural network. This brings up an important distinction.

The human brain is more accurately described as a biological neural network (BNN). This book is not about biological neural networks. This book is about artificial neural networks (ANN). Most texts do not make the distinction between the two. Throughout this text, references to neural networks imply artificial neural networks.

There are some basic similarities between biological neural networks and artificial neural networks. Artificial neural networks are largely mathematical constructs that were inspired by biological neural networks. An important term that is often used to describe various artificial neural network algorithms is "biological plausibility." This term defines how close an artificial neural network algorithm is to a biological neural network.

As stated earlier, neural networks are designed to accomplish one small task. A full application likely uses neural networks to accomplish certain parts of its objectives. The entire application is not be implemented as a neural network. The application may be made of several neural networks, each designed for a specific task.

The neural networks accomplish pattern recognition tasking very well. When communicated a pattern, a neural network communicates that pattern back. At the highest level, this is all that a typical neural network does. Some network architectures will vary this, but the vast majority of neural networks work this way. Figure 1 illustrates a neural network at this level.

Figure 1: A Typical Neural Network

As you can see, the neural network above is accepting a pattern and returning a pattern. Neural networks operate completely synchronously. A neural network will only output when presented with input. It is not like a human brain, which does not operate exactly synchronously. The human brain responds to input, but it will produce output anytime it desires!

0.2.1   Neural Network Structure

Neural networks are made of layers of similar neurons. At minimum, most neural networks consist of an input layer and output layer. The input pattern is presented to the input layer. Then the output pattern is returned from the output layer. What happens between the input and output layers is a black box. At this point in the book, the neural network's internal structure is not yet a concern. There are many architectures that define interactions between the input and output layer. Later in this book, these architectures are examined.

The input and output patterns are both arrays of floating point numbers. An example of these patterns follows.

```
Neural Network Input:  [ -0.245, .283, 0.0 ]
Neural Network Output: [ 0.782, 0.543 ]
```

The neural network above has three neurons in the input layer and two neurons in the output layer. The number of neurons in the input and output layers do not change. As a result, the number of elements in the input and output patterns, for a particular neural network, can never change.

To make use of the neural network, problem input must be expressed as an array of floating point numbers. Likewise, the problem's solution must be an array of floating point numbers. This is the essential and only true value of a neural network. Neural networks take one array and transform it into a second. Neural networks do not loop, call subroutines, or perform any of the other tasks associated with traditional programming. Neural networks recognize patterns.

A neural network is much like a hash table in traditional programming. A hash table is used to map keys to values, somewhat like a dictionary. The following could be thought of as a hash table:

- "hear" -> "to perceive or apprehend by the ear"

- "run" -> "to go faster than a walk"

- "write" -> "to form (as characters or symbols) on a surface with an instrument (as a pen)"

This is a mapping between words and the definition of each word, or a hash table just as in any programming language. It uses a string key to another value of a string. Input is the dictionary with a key and output is a value. This is how most neural networks function. One neural network called a Bidirectional Associative Memory (BAM) actually allows a user to also pass in the value and receive the key.

Hash tables use keys and values. Think of the pattern sent to the neural network's input layer as the key to the hash table. Likewise, think of the value returned from the hash table as the pattern returned from the neural network's output layer. The comparison between a hash table and a neural network works well; however, the neural network is much more than a hash table.

What would happen with the above hash table if a word was passed that was not a map key? For example, pass in the key "wrote." A hash table would return **null** or indicate in some way that it could not find the specified key. Neural networks do not return null, but rather find the closest match. Not only do they find the closest match, neural networks modify the output to estimate the missing value. So if "wrote" is passed to the neural network above, the output would likely be "write." There is not enough data for the neural network to have modified the response, as there are only three samples. So you would likely get the output from one of the other keys.

The above mapping brings up one very important point about neural networks. Recall that neural networks accept an array of floating point numbers and return another array. How would strings be put into the neural network as seen above? While there are ways to do this, it is much easier to deal with numeric data than strings.

With a neural network problem, inputs must be arrays of floating point numbers. This is one of the most difficult aspects of neural network programming. How are problems translated into a fixed-length array of floating point numbers? The best way is by demonstration. Examples are explored throughout the remainder of this introduction.

0.2.2   A Simple Example

Most basic literature concerning neural networks provide examples with the XOR operator. The XOR operator is essentially the "Hello World" of neural network programming. While this book will describe scenarios much more complex than XOR, the XOR operator is a great introduction.

To begin, view the XOR operator as though it were a hash table. XOR operators work similar to the AND and OR operators. For an AND to be **true**, both sides must be **true**. For an OR to be **true**, either side must be **true**. For an XOR to be **true**, both of the sides must be different from each other. The truth table for an XOR is as follows.

```
False XOR False = False
True XOR False = True
False XOR True = True
True XOR True = False
```

To continue the hash table example, the above truth table would be represented as follows.

```
[ 0.0 , 0.0 ] -> [ 0.0 ]
[ 1.0 , 0.0 ] -> [ 1.0 ]
[ 0.0 , 1.0 ] -> [ 1.0 ]
[ 1.0 , 1.0 ] -> [ 0.0 ]
```

These mapping show input and the ideal expected output for the neural network.

0.3   When to use Neural Networks

With neural networks defined, it must be determined when or when not to use them. Knowing when not to use something is just as important as knowing how to use it. To understand these objectives, we will identify what sort of problems Encog is adept at solving.

A significant goal of this book is explain how to construct Encog neural networks and when to use them. Neural network programmers must understand which problems are well-suited for neural network solutions and which are not. An effective neural network programmer also knows which neural network structure, if any, is most applicable to a given problem. This section begins by identifying which problems that are not conducive to a neural network solution.

0.3.1   Problems Not Suited to a Neural Network Solution

Programs that are easily written as flowcharts are not ideal applications for neural networks. If your program consists of well-defined steps, normal programming techniques will suffice.

Another criterion to consider is whether program logic is likely to change. One of the primary features of neural networks is the ability to learn. If the algorithm used to solve your problem is an unchanging business rule, there is no reason to use a neural network. In fact, a neural network might be detrimental to your application if it attempts to find a better solution and begins to diverge from the desired process. Unexpected results will likely occur.

Finally, neural networks are often not suitable for problems that require a clearly traceable path to solution. A neural network can be very useful for solving the problem for which it was trained, but cannot explain its reasoning. The neural network knows something because it was trained to know it. However, a neural network cannot explain the series of steps followed to derive the answer.

0.3.2   Problems Suited to a Neural Network

Although there are many problems for which neural networks are not well suited, there are also many problems for which a neural network solution is quite useful. In addition, neural networks can often solve problems with fewer lines of code than traditional programming algorithms. It is important to understand which problems call for a neural network approach.

Neural networks are particularly useful for solving problems that cannot be expressed as a series of steps. This may include recognizing patterns, classification, series prediction and data mining.

Pattern recognition is perhaps the most common use for neural networks. For this type of problem, the neural network is presented a pattern in the form of an image, a sound or other data. The neural network then attempts to determine if the input data matches a pattern that it has been trained to recognize. The remainder of this textbook will examine many examples of how to use neural networks to recognize patterns.

Classification is a process that is closely related to pattern recognition. A neural network trained for classification is designed to classify input samples into groups. These groups may be fuzzy and lack clearly-defined boundaries. Alternatively, these groups may have quite rigid boundaries.

0.4   Structure of the Book

This book begins with Chapter 1, "Regression, Classification & Clustering." This chapter introduces the major tasks performed with neural networks. These tasks are not just performed by neural networks, but also by many other machine learning methods as well.

One of the primary tasks for neural networks is to recognize and provide insight into data. Chapter 2, "Obtaining Data & Normalization," shows how to process this data before using a neural network. This chapter will examine some data that might be used with a neural network and how to normalize and use this data with a neural network.

Encog includes a GUI neural network editor called the Encog Workbench. Chapter 3, "Using the Encog Workbench," details the best methods and uses for this application. The Encog Workbench provides a GUI tool that can edit the .EG data files used by the Encog Framework. The powerful Encog Analyst can also be used to automate many tasks.

The next step is to construct and save neural networks. Chapter 4, "Constructing Neural Networks in Java," shows how to create neural networks using layers and activation functions. It will also illustrate how to save neural networks to either platform-independent .EG files or standard Java serialization.

Neural networks must be trained for effective utilization and there are several ways to perform this training. Chapter 5, "Propagation Training," shows how to use the propagation methods built into Encog to train neural networks. Encog supports backpropagation, resilient propagation, the Manhattan update rule, Quick Propagation and SCG.

Chapter 6, "Other Supervised Training Methods," shows other supervised training algorithms supported by Encog. This chapter introduces simulated annealing and genetic algorithms as training techniques for Encog networks. Chapter 6 also details how to create hybrid training algorithms.

Feedforward neural networks are not the only type supported by Encog. Chapter 7, "Other Neural Network Types," provides a brief introduction to several other neural network types that Encog supports well. Chapter 7 describes how to setup NEAT, ART1 and Elman/Jordan neural networks.

Neural networks are commonly used to predict future data changes. One common use for this is to predict stock market trends. Chapter 8, "Using Temporal Data," will show how to use Encog to predict trends.

Images are frequently used as an input for neural networks. Encog contains classes that make it easy to use image data to feed and train neural networks. Chapter 9, "Using Image Data," shows how to use image data with Encog.

Finally, Chapter 10, "Using Self Organizing Maps," expands beyond supervised training to explain how to use unsupervised training with Encog. A Self Organizing Map (SOM) can be used to cluster data.

As you read though this book you will undoubtedly have questions about the Encog Framework. Your best resources are the Encog forums at Heaton Research, found at the following URL.

http://www.heatonresearch.com/forum

Additionally, the Encog Wiki, located at the following URL.

http://www.heatonresearch.com/wiki/Main_Page

Chapter 1

Regression, Classification & Clustering

- Classifying Data

- Regression Analysis of Data

- Clustering Data

- How Machine Learning Problems are Structured

While there are other models, regression, classification and clustering are the three primary ways that data is evaluated for machine learning problems. These three models are the most common and the focus of this book. The next sections will introduce you to classification, regression and clustering.

1.1   Data Classification

Classification attempts to determine what class the input data falls into. Classification is usually a supervised training operation, meaning the user provides data and expected results to the neural network. For data classification, the expected result is identification of the data class.

Supervised neural networks are always trained with known data. During training, the networks are evaluated on how well they classify known data. The hope is that the neural network, once trained, will be able to classify unknown data as well.

Fisher's Iris Dataset is an example of classification. This is a dataset that contains measurements of Iris flowers. This is one of the most famous datasets and is often used to evaluate machine learning methods. The full dataset is available at the following URL.

http://www.heatonresearch.com/wiki/Iris_Data_Set

Below is small sampling from the Iris data set.

```
"Sepal Length","Sepal Width","Petal Length","Petal Width","Species
    "
5.1,3.5,1.4,0.2,"setosa"
4.9,3.0,1.4,0.2,"setosa"
4.7,3.2,1.3,0.2,"setosa"
...
7.0,3.2,4.7,1.4,"versicolor"
6.4,3.2,4.5,1.5,"versicolor"
6.9,3.1,4.9,1.5,"versicolor"
...
6.3,3.3,6.0,2.5,"virginica"
5.8,2.7,5.1,1.9,"virginica"
7.1,3.0,5.9,2.1,"virginica"
```

The above data is shown as a CSV file. CSV is a very common input format for a neural network. The first row is typically a definition for each of the columns in the file. As you can see, for each of the flowers there are five pieces of information are provided.

- Sepal Length

- Sepal Width

- Petal Length

- Petal Width

- Species

For classification, the neural network is instructed that, given the sepal length-/width and the petal length/width, the species of the flower can be determined. The species is the class.

A class is usually a non-numeric data attribute and as such, membership in the class must be well-defined. For the Iris data set, there are three different types of Iris. If a neural network is trained on three types of Iris, it cannot be expected to identify a rose. All members of the class must be known at the time of training.

1.2   Regression Analysis

In the last section, we learned how to use data to classify data. Often the desired output is not simply a class, but a number. Consider the calculation of an automobile's miles per gallon (MPG). Provided data such as the engine size and car weight, the MPG for the specified car may be calculated.

Consider the following sample data for five cars:

```
"mpg","cylinders","displacement","horsepower","weight","
    acceleration","model year","origin","car name"
18.0,8,307.0,130.0,3504.,12.0,70,1,"chevrolet chevelle malibu"
15.0,8,350.0,165.0,3693.,11.5,70,1,"buick skylark 320"
18.0,8,318.0,150.0,3436.,11.0,70,1,"plymouth satellite"
16.0,8,304.0,150.0,3433.,12.0,70,1,"amc rebel sst"
17.0,8,302.0,140.0,3449.,10.5,70,1,"ford torino"
...
```

For more information, the entirety of this dataset may be found at:

http://www.heatonresearch.com/wiki/MPG_Data_Set

The idea of regression is to train the neural network with input data about the car. However, using regression, the network will not produce a class. The neural network is expected to provide the miles per gallon that the specified car would likely get.

It is also important to note that not use every piece of data in the above file will be used. The columns "car name" and "origin" are not used. The name of a car has nothing to do with its fuel efficiency and is therefore excluded. Likewise the origin does not contribute to this equation. The origin is a numeric value that specifies what geographic region the car was produced in. While some regions do focus on fuel efficiency, this piece of data is far too broad to be useful.

1.3   Clustering

Another common type of analysis is clustering. Unlike the previous two analysis types, clustering is typically unsupervised. Either of the datasets from the previous two sections could be used for clustering. The difference is that clustering analysis would not require the user to provide the species in the case of the Iris dataset, or the MPG number for the MPG dataset. The clustering algorithm is expected to place the data elements into clusters that correspond to the species or MPG.

For clustering, the machine learning method simply looks at the data and attempts to place that data into a number of clusters. The number of clusters expected must be defined ahead of time. If the number of clusters changes, the clustering machine learning method will need to be retrained.

Clustering is very similar to classification, with its output being a cluster, which is similar to a class. However, clustering differs from regression as it does not provide a number. So if clustering were used with the MPG dataset, the output would need to be a cluster that the car falls into. Perhaps each cluster would specify the varying level of fuel efficiency for the vehicle. Perhaps the clusters would group the cars into clusters that demonstrated some relationship that had not yet been noticed.

1.4   Structuring a Neural Network

Now the three major problem models for neural networks are identified, it is time to examine how data is actually presented to the neural network. This section focuses mainly on how the neural network is structured to accept data items and provide output. The following chapter will detail how to normalize the data prior to being presented to the neural network.

Neural networks are typically layered with an input and output layer at minimum. There may also be hidden layers. Some neural network types are not broken up into any formal layers beyond the input and output layer. However, the input layer and output layer will always be present and may be incorporated in the same layer. We will now examine the input layer, output layer and hidden layers.

1.4.1 Understanding the Input Layer

The input layer is the first layer in a neural network. This layer, like all layers, contains a specific number of neurons. The neurons in a layer all contain similar properties. Typically, the input layer will have one neuron for each attribute that the neural network will use for classification, regression or clustering.

Consider the previous examples. The Iris dataset has four input neurons. These neurons represent the petal width/length and the sepal width/length. The MPG dataset has more input neurons. The number of input neurons does not always directly correspond to the number of attributes and some attributes will take more than one neuron to encode. This encoding process, called normalization, will be covered in the next chapter.

The number of neurons determines how a layer's input is structured. For each input neuron, one **double** value is stored. For example, the following array could be used as input to a layer that contained five neurons.

```
double[] input = new double[5];
```

The input to a neural network is always an array of the type **double**. The size of this array directly corresponds to the number of neurons on the input layer. Encog uses the **MLData** interface to define classes that hold these arrays. The array above can be easily converted into an **MLData** object with the following line of code.

```
MLData data = new BasicMLData(input);
```

The **MLData** interface defines any "array like" data that may be presented to Encog. Input must always be presented to the neural network inside of a

MLData object. The **BasicMLData** class implements the **MLData** interface. However, the **BasicMLData** class is not the only way to provide Encog with data. Other implementations of **MLData** are used for more specialized types of data.

The **BasicMLData** class simply provides a memory-based data holder for the neural network data. Once the neural network processes the input, a **MLData**-based class will be returned from the neural network's output layer. The output layer is discussed in the next section.

1.4.2   Understanding the Output Layer

The output layer is the final layer in a neural network. This layer provides the output after all previous layers have processed the input. The output from the output layer is formatted very similarly to the data that was provided to the input layer. The neural network outputs an array of doubles.

The neural network wraps the output in a class based on the **MLData** interface. Most of the built-in neural network types return a **BasicMLData** class as the output. However, future and third party neural network classes may return different classes based other implementations of the **MLData** interface.

Neural networks are designed to accept input (an array of doubles) and then produce output (also an array of doubles). Determining how to structure the input data and attaching meaning to the output are the two main challenges of adapting a problem to a neural network. The real power of a neural network comes from its pattern recognition capabilities. The neural network should be able to produce the desired output even if the input has been slightly distorted.

Regression neural networks typically produce a single output neuron that provides the numeric value produced by the neural network. Multiple output neurons may exist if the same neural network is supposed to predict two or more numbers for the given inputs.

Classification produce one or more output neurons, depending on how the output class was encoded. There are several different ways to encode classes. This will be discussed in greater detail in the next chapter.

Clustering is setup similarly as the output neurons identify which data belongs to what cluster.

1.4.3 Hidden Layers

As previously discussed, neural networks contain and input layer and an output layer. Sometimes the input layer and output layer are the same, but are most often two separate layers. Additionally, other layers may exist between the input and output layers and are called hidden layers. These hidden layers are simply inserted between the input and output layers. The hidden layers can also take on more complex structures.

The only purpose of the hidden layers is to allow the neural network to better produce the expected output for the given input. Neural network programming involves first defining the input and output layer neuron counts. Once it is determined how to translate the programming problem into the input and output neuron counts, it is time to define the hidden layers.

The hidden layers are very much a "black box." The problem is defined in terms of the neuron counts for the hidden and output layers. How the neural network produces the correct output is performed in part by hidden layers. Once the structure of the input and output layers is defined, the hidden layer structure that optimally learns the problem must also be defined.

The challenge is to avoid creating a hidden structure that is either too complex or too simple. Too complex of a hidden structure will take too long to train. Too simple of a hidden structure will not learn the problem. A good starting point is a single hidden layer with a number of neurons equal to twice the input layer. Depending on this network's performance, the hidden layer's number of neurons is either increased or decreased.

Developers often wonder how many hidden layers to use. Some research has indicated that a second hidden layer is rarely of any value. Encog is an excellent way to perform a trial and error search for the most optimal hidden layer configuration. For more information see the following URL:

http://www.heatonresearch.com/wiki/Hidden_Layers

Some neural networks have no hidden layers, with the input layer directly connected to the output layer. Further, some neural networks have only a single layer in which the single layer is self-connected. These connections permit the network to learn. Contained in these connections, called synapses, are individual weight matrixes. These values are changed as the neural network learns. The next chapter delves more into weight matrixes.

1.5   Using a Neural Network

This section will detail how to structure a neural network for a very simple problem: to design a neural network that can function as an XOR operator. Learning the XOR operator is a frequent "first example" when demonstrating the architecture of a new neural network. Just as most new programming languages are first demonstrated with a program that simply displays "Hello World," neural networks are frequently demonstrated with the XOR operator. Learning the XOR operator is sort of the "Hello World" application for neural networks.

1.5.1   The XOR Operator and Neural Networks

The XOR operator is one of common Boolean logical operators. The other two are the AND and OR operators. For each of these logical operators, there are four different combinations. All possible combinations for the AND operator are shown below.

```
0 AND 0 = 0
1 AND 0 = 0
0 AND 1 = 0
1 AND 1 = 1
```

This should be consistent with how you learned the AND operator for computer programming. As its name implies, the AND operator will only return **true**, or one, when both inputs are **true**.

The OR operator behaves as follows:

```
0 OR 0 = 0
1 OR 0 = 1
0 OR 1 = 1
1 OR 1 = 1
```

This also should be consistent with how you learned the OR operator for computer programming. For the OR operator to be **true**, either of the inputs must be **true**.

The "exclusive or" (XOR) operator is less frequently used in computer programming. XOR has the same output as the OR operator, except for the case where both inputs are **true**. The possible combinations for the XOR operator are shown here.

```
0 XOR 0 = 0
1 XOR 0 = 1
0 XOR 1 = 1
1 XOR 1 = 0
```

As you can see, the XOR operator only returns **true** when both inputs differ. The next section explains how to structure the input, output and hidden layers for the XOR operator.

1.5.2   Structuring a Neural Network for XOR

There are two inputs to the XOR operator and one output. The input and output layers will be structured accordingly. The input neurons are fed the following **double** values:

```
0.0 ,0.0
1.0 ,0.0
0.0 ,1.0
1.0 ,1.0
```

These values correspond to the inputs to the XOR operator, shown above. The one output neuron is expected to produce the following **double** values:

```
0.0
1.0
```

```
1.0
0.0
```

This is one way that the neural network can be structured. This method allows a simple feedforward neural network to learn the XOR operator. The feedforward neural network, also called a perceptron, is one of the first neural network architectures that we will learn.

There are other ways that the XOR data could be presented to the neural network. Later in this book, two examples of recurrent neural networks will be explored including Elman and Jordan styles of neural networks. These methods would treat the XOR data as one long sequence, basically concatenating the truth table for XOR together, resulting in one long XOR sequence, such as:

```
0.0 ,0.0 ,0.0 ,
0.0 ,1.0 ,1.0 ,
1.0 ,0.0 ,1.0 ,
1.0 ,1.0 ,0.0
```

The line breaks are only for readability; the neural network treats XOR as a long sequence. By using the data above, the network has a single input neuron and a single output neuron. The input neuron is fed one value from the list above and the output neuron is expected to return the next value.

This shows that there are often multiple ways to model the data for a neural network. How the data is modeled will greatly influence the success of a neural network. If one particular model is not working, another should be considered. The next step is to format the XOR data for a feedforward neural network.

Because the XOR operator has two inputs and one output, the neural network follows suit. Additionally, the neural network has a single hidden layer with two neurons to help process the data. The choice for two neurons in the hidden layer is arbitrary and often results in trial and error. The XOR problem is simple and two hidden neurons are sufficient to solve it. A diagram for this network is shown in Figure 1.1.

Figure 1.1: Neuron Diagram for the XOR Network

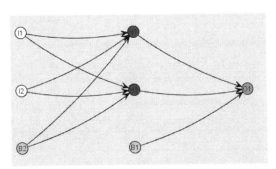

There are four different types of neurons in the above network. These are summarized below:

- Input Neurons: I1, I2

- Output Neuron: O1

- Hidden Neurons: H1, H2

- Bias Neurons: B1, B2

The input, output and hidden neurons were discussed previously. The new neuron type seen in this diagram is the bias neuron. A bias neuron always outputs a value of 1 and never receives input from the previous layer.

In a nutshell, bias neurons allow the neural network to learn patterns more effectively. They serve a similar function to the hidden neurons. Without bias neurons, it is very hard for the neural network to output a value of one when the input is zero. This is not so much a problem for XOR data, but it can be for other data sets. To read more about their exact function, visit the following URL:

http://www.heatonresearch.com/wiki/Bias

Now look at the code used to produce a neural network that solves the XOR operator. The complete code is included with the Encog examples and can be found at the following location.

```
org.encog.examples.neural.xor.XORHelloWorld
```

The example begins by creating the neural network seen in Figure 1.1. The code needed to create this network is relatively simple:

```
BasicNetwork network = new BasicNetwork();
network.addLayer(new BasicLayer(null,true,2));
network.addLayer(new BasicLayer(new ActivationSigmoid(),true,3));
network.addLayer(new BasicLayer(new ActivationSigmoid(),false,1));
network.getStructure().finalizeStructure();
network.reset();
```

In the above code, a **BasicNetwork** is being created. Three layers are added to this network. The first layer, which becomes the input layer, has two neurons. The hidden layer is added second and has two neurons also. Lastly, the output layer is added and has a single neuron. Finally, the **finalizeStructure** method is called to inform the network that no more layers are to be added. The call to **reset** randomizes the weights in the connections between these layers.

Neural networks always begin with random weight values. A process called training refines these weights to values that will provide the desired output. Because neural networks always start with random values, very different results occur from two runs of the same program. Some random weights provide a better starting point than others. Sometimes random weights will be far enough off that the network will fail to learn. In this case, the weights should be randomized again and the process restarted.

You will also notice the **ActivationSigmoid** class in the above code. This specifies the neural network to use the sigmoid activation function. Activation functions will be covered in Chapter 4. The activation functions are only placed on the hidden and output layer; the input layer does not have an activation function. If an activation function were specified for the input layer, it would have no effect.

Each layer also specifies a **boolean** value. This **boolean** value specifies if bias neurons are present on a layer or not. The output layer, as shown in Figure 1.1, does not have a bias neuron as input and hidden layers do. This is because a bias neuron is only connected to the next layer. The output layer is the final layer, so there is no need for a bias neuron. If a bias neuron was specified on the output layer, it would have no effect.

These weights make up the long-term memory of the neural network. Some neural networks also contain context layers which give the neural network a short-term memory as well. The neural network learns by modifying these weight values. This is also true of the Elman and Jordan neural networks.

Now that the neural network has been created, it must be trained. Training is the process where the random weights are refined to produce output closer to the desired output. Training is discussed in the next section.

1.5.3   Training a Neural Network

To train the neural network, a **MLDataSet** object is constructed. This object contains the inputs and the expected outputs. To construct this object, two arrays are created. The first array will hold the input values for the XOR operator. The second array will hold the ideal outputs for each of four corresponding input values. These will correspond to the possible values for XOR. To review, the four possible values are as follows:

```
0 XOR 0 = 0
1 XOR 0 = 1
0 XOR 1 = 1
1 XOR 1 = 0
```

First, construct an array to hold the four input values to the XOR operator using a two dimensional **double** array. This array is as follows:

```
public static double XOR_INPUT [][] = {
{ 0.0, 0.0 },
{ 1.0, 0.0 },
{ 0.0, 1.0 },
{ 1.0, 1.0 } };
```

Likewise, an array must be created for the expected outputs for each of the input values. This array is as follows:

```
public static double XOR_IDEAL [][] = {
{ 0.0 },
{ 1.0 },
{ 1.0 },
```

```
{ 0.0 } };
```

Even though there is only one output value, a two-dimensional array must still be used to represent the output. If there is more than one output neuron, additional columns are added to the array.

Now that the two input arrays are constructed, a **MLDataSet** object must be created to hold the training set. This object is created as follows:

```
MLDataSet trainingSet = new BasicMLDataSet(XOR_INPUT, XOR_IDEAL);
```

Now that the training set has been created, the neural network can be trained. Training is the process where the neural network's weights are adjusted to better produce the expected output. Training will continue for many iterations until the error rate of the network is below an acceptable level. First, a training object must be created. Encog supports many different types of training.

For this example Resilient Propagation (RPROP) training is used. RPROP is perhaps the best general-purpose training algorithm supported by Encog. Other training techniques are provided as well as certain problems are solved better with certain training techniques. The following code constructs a RPROP trainer:

```
MLTrain train = new ResilientPropagation(network, trainingSet);
```

All training classes implement the **MLTrain** interface. The RPROP algorithm is implemented by the **ResilientPropagation** class, which is constructed above.

Once the trainer is constructed, the neural network should be trained. Training the neural network involves calling the **iteration** method on the **MLTrain** class until the error is below a specific value. The error is the degree to which the neural network output matches the desired output.

```
int epoch = 1;
do {
   train.iteration();
   System.out.println("Epoch #" + epoch + " Error:"
     + train.getError());
   epoch++;
} while(train.getError() > 0.01);
```

The above code loops through as many iterations, or epochs, as it takes to get the error rate for the neural network to be below 1%. Once the neural network has been trained, it is ready for use. The next section will explain how to use a neural network.

1.5.4   Executing a Neural Network

Making use of the neural network involves calling the **compute** method on the **BasicNetwork** class. Here we loop through every training set value and display the output from the neural network:

```
System.out.println("Neural Network Results:");
for(MLDataPair pair: trainingSet ) {
  final MLData output =
    network.compute(pair.getInput());
  System.out.println(pair.getInput().getData(0)
    + "," + pair.getInput().getData(1)
    + ", actual=" + output.getData(0) + ",ideal=" +
  pair.getIdeal().getData(0));
}
```

The **compute** method accepts an **MLData** class and also returns another **MLData** object. The returned object contains the output from the neural network, which is displayed to the user. With the program run, the training results are first displayed. For each epoch, the current error rate is displayed.

```
Epoch #1  Error:0.5604437512295236
Epoch #2  Error:0.5056375155784316
Epoch #3  Error:0.5026960720526166
Epoch #4  Error:0.4907299498390594

...
Epoch #104  Error:0.01017278345766472
Epoch #105  Error:0.010557202078697751
Epoch #106  Error:0.011034965164672806
Epoch #107  Error:0.009682102808616387
```

The error starts at 56% at epoch 1. By epoch 107, the training dropped below 1% and training stops. Because neural network was initialized with random weights, it may take different numbers of iterations to train each time the program is run. Additionally, though the final error rate may be different, it should always end below 1%.

Finally, the program displays the results from each of the training items as follows:

```
Neural Network Results:
0.0,0.0,  actual=0.002782538818034049,ideal=0.0
1.0,0.0,  actual=0.9903741937121177,ideal=1.0
0.0,1.0,  actual=0.9836807956566187,ideal=1.0
1.0,1.0,  actual=0.0011646072586172778,ideal=0.0
```

As you can see, the network has not been trained to give the exact results. This is normal. Because the network was trained to 1% error, each of the results will also be within generally 1% of the expected value.

Because the neural network is initialized to random values, the final output will be different on second run of the program.

```
Neural Network Results:
0.0,0.0,  actual=0.005489822214926685,ideal=0.0
1.0,0.0,  actual=0.985425090860287,ideal=1.0
0.0,1.0,  actual=0.9888064742994463,ideal=1.0
1.0,1.0,  actual=0.005923146369557053,ideal=0.0
```

The second run output is slightly different. This is normal.

This is the first Encog example. All of the examples contained in this book are also included with the examples downloaded with Encog. For more information on how to download these examples and where this particular example is located, refer to Appendix A, "Installing Encog."

1.6 Chapter Summary

Encog is an advanced machine learning framework used to create neural networks. This chapter focused on regression in classification and clustering. Finally, this chapter showed how to create an Encog application that could learn the XOR operator.

Regression is when a neural network accepts input and produces a numeric output. Classification is where a neural network accepts input and predicts what class the input was in. Clustering does not require ideal outputs. Rather, clustering looks at the input data and clusters the input cases as best it can.

There are several different layer types supported by Encog. However, these layers fall into three groups depending their placement in the neural network. The input layer accepts input from the outside. Hidden layers accept data from the input layer for further processing. The output layer takes data, either from the input or final hidden layer, and presents it on to the outside world.

The XOR operator was used as an example for this chapter. The XOR operator is frequently used as a simple "Hello World" application for neural networks. The XOR operator provides a very simple pattern that most neural networks can easily learn. It is important to know how to structure data for a neural network. Neural networks both accept and return an array of floating point numbers.

Finally, this chapter detailed how to send data to a neural network. Data for the XOR example is easily provided to a neural network. No normalization or encoding is necessary. However, most real world data will need to be normalized. Normalization is demonstrated in the next chapter.

Chapter 2

Obtaining Data for Encog

- Finding Data for Neural Networks

- Why Normalize?

- Specifying Normalization Sources

- Specifying Normalization Targets

Neural networks can provide profound insights into the data supplied to them. However, you can't just feed any sort of data directly into a neural network. This "raw" data must usually be normalized into a form that the neural network can process. This chapter will show how to normalize "raw" data for use by Encog.

Before data can be normalized, we must first have data. Once you decide what the neural network should do, you must find data to teach the neural network how to perform a task. Fortunately, the Internet provides a wealth of information that can be used with neural networks.

2.1 Where to Get Data for Neural Networks

The Internet can be a great source of data for the neural network. Data found on the Internet can be in many different formats. One of the most convenient formats for data is the comma-separated value (CSV) format. Other times it may be necessary to create a spider or bot to obtain this data.

One very useful source for neural network is the Machine Learning Repository, which is run by the University of California at Irvine.

http://kdd.ics.uci.edu/

The Machine Learning Repository site is a repository of various datasets that have been donated to the University of California. Several of these datasets will be used in this book.

2.2   Normalizing Data

Data obtained from sites, such as those listed above, often cannot be directly fed into neural networks. Neural networks can be very "intelligent," but cannot receive just any sort of data and produce a meaningful result. Often the data must first be normalized. We will begin by defining normalization.

Neural networks are designed to accept floating-point numbers as their input. Usually these input numbers should be in either the range of -1 to +1 or 0 to +1 for maximum efficiency. The choice of which range is often dictated by the choice of activation function, as certain activation functions have a positive range and others have both a negative and positive range.

The sigmoid activation function, for example, has a range of only positive numbers. Conversely, the hyperbolic tangent activation function has a range of positive and negative numbers. The most common case is to use a hyperbolic tangent activation function with a normalization range of -1 to +1.

Recall from Chapter 1 the iris dataset. This data set could be applied to a classification problem. However, we did not see how the data needed to be actually processed to make it useful to a neural network.

A sampling of the dataset is shown here:

```
"Sepal Length","Sepal Width","Petal Length","Petal Width","Species
     "
5.1,3.5,1.4,0.2,"setosa"
4.9,3.0,1.4,0.2,"setosa"
4.7,3.2,1.3,0.2,"setosa"
...
```

```
7.0 ,3.2 ,4.7 ,1.4 ," versicolor "
6.4 ,3.2 ,4.5 ,1.5 ," versicolor "
6.9 ,3.1 ,4.9 ,1.5 ," versicolor "
...
6.3 ,3.3 ,6.0 ,2.5 ," virginica "
5.8 ,2.7 ,5.1 ,1.9 ," virginica "
7.1 ,3.0 ,5.9 ,2.1 ," virginica "
```

The fields from this dataset must now be represented as an array of floating point numbers between -1 and +1.

- Sepal Length - Numeric

- Sepal Width - Numeric

- Petal Length - Numeric

- Petal Width - Numeric

- Species - Class

There are really two different attribute types to consider. First, there are four numeric attributes. Each of these will simply map to an input neuron. The values will need to be scaled to -1 to +1.

Class attributes, sometimes called nominal attributes, present a unique challenge. In the example, the species of iris must be represented as either one or more floating point numbers. The mapping will not be to a single neuron. Because a three-member class is involved, the number of neurons used to represent the species will not be a single neuron. The number of neurons used to represent the species will be either two or three, depending on the normalization type used.

The next two sections will show how to normalize numeric and class values, beginning with numeric values.

2.2.1   Normalizing Numeric Values

Normalizing a numeric value is essentially a process of mapping the existing numeric value to well-defined numeric range, such as -1 to +1. Normalization causes all of the attributes to be in the same range with no one attribute more powerful than the others.

To normalize, the current numeric ranges must be known for all of the attributes. The current numeric ranges for each of the iris attributes are shown here.

- Sepal Length - Max: 7.9, Min: 4.3

- Sepal Width - Max: 4.4, Min: 2.0

- Petal Length - Max: 6.9, Min: 1.0

- Petal Width - Max: 2.5, Min: 0.1

Consider the "Petal Length." The petal length is in the range of 1.0 to 6.9. This must convert this length to -1 to +1. To do this we use Equation 2.1.

$$f(x) = \frac{(x - d_L)(n_H - n_L)}{(d_H - d_L)} + n_L \qquad (2.1)$$

The above equation will normalize a value **x**, where the variable **d** represents the high and low values of the data, the variable **n** represents the high and low normalization range desired. For example, to normalize a petal length of 3, to the range -1 to +1, the above equation becomes:

$$f(x) = \frac{(3 - 1.0)(1.0 - (-1.0))}{(6.9 - 1.0)} + (-1.0) \qquad (2.2)$$

This results in a value of 0.66. This is the value that will be fed to the neural network.

For regression, the neural network will return values. These values will be normalized. To denormalize a value, Equation 2.2 is used.

$$f(x) = \frac{(d_L - d_H)x - (n_H \cdot d_L) + d_H \cdot n_L}{(n_L - n_H)} \qquad (2.3)$$

To denormalize the value of 0.66, Equation 2.2 becomes:

$$f(x) = \frac{(1.0 - 6.9) \cdot 0.32 - (1.0 \cdot 1.0) + 6.9 \cdot -1}{((-1) - (1.0))} \qquad (2.4)$$

Once denormalized, the value of 0.66 becomes 2.0 again. It is important to note that the 0.66 value was rounded for the calculation here. Encog provides built-in classes to provide both normalization and denormalization. These classes will be introduced later in this chapter.

2.2.2 Normalizing Nominal Values

Nominal values are used to name things. One very common example of a simple nominal value is gender. Something is either male or female. Another is any sort of Boolean question. Nominal values also include values that are either "yes/true" or "no/false." However, not all nominal values have only two values.

Nominal values can also be used to describe an attribute of something, such as color. Neural networks deal best with nominal values where the set is fixed. For the iris dataset, the nominal value to be normalized is the species. There are three different species to consider for the iris dataset and this value cannot change. If the neural network is trained with three species, it cannot be expected to recognize five species.

Encog supports two different ways to encode nominal values. The simplest means of representing nominal values is called "one-of-n" encoding. One-of-n encoding can often be hard to train, especially if there are more than a few nominal types to encode. Equilateral encoding is usually a better choice than the simpler one-of-n encoding. Both encoding types will be explored in the next two sections.

2.2.3   Understanding One-of-n Normalization

One-of-n is a very simple form of normalization. For an example, consider the iris dataset again. The input to the neural network is statistics about an individual iris. The output signifies which species of iris to evaluate. The three iris species are listed as follows:

- Setosa

- Versicolor

- Virginica

If using the one-of-n normalization, the neural network would have three output neurons. Each of these three neurons would represent one iris species. The iris species predicted by the neural network would correspond to the output neuron with the highest activation.

Generating training data for one-of-n is relatively easy. Simply assign a +1 to the neuron that corresponds to the chosen iris and a -1 to the remaining neurons. For example, the Setosa iris species would be encoded as follows:

```
1,−1,−1
```

Likewise, the Versicolor would be encoded as follows:

```
−1,1,−1
```

Finally, Virginica would be encoded as follows.

```
−1,−1,1
```

Encog provides built-in classes to provide this normalization. These classes will be introduced later in this chapter.

2.2.4   Understanding Equilateral Normalization

The output neurons are constantly checked against the ideal output values
provided in the training set. The error between the actual output and the
ideal output is represented by a percentage. This can cause a problem for the
one-of-n normalization method. Consider if the neural network had predicted
a Versicolor iris when it should have predicted a Verginica iris. The actual
output and ideal would be as follows:

```
Ideal  Output:   -1, -1,   1
Actual Output:   -1,   1, -1
```

The problem is that only two of three output neurons are incorrect. We would
like to spread the "guilt" for this error over a larger percent of the neurons.
To do this, a unique set of values for each class must be determined. Each set
of values should have an equal Euclidean distance from the others. The equal
distance makes sure that incorrectly choosing iris Setosa for Versicolor has the
same error weight as choosing iris Setosa for iris Virginica.

   This can be done using the **Equilateral** class. The following code segment
shows how to use the **Equilateral** class to generate these values:

```java
Equilateral eq = new Equilateral(3,-1,1);
for(int i=0;i<3;i++) {
  StringBuilder line = new StringBuilder();
  line.append(i);
line.append(':');
double[] d = eq.encode(i);
  for(int j=0;j<d.length;j++)
  {
    if( j>0 )
      line.append(',');
    line.append(Format.formatDouble(d[j],4));
  }
  System.out.println(line.toString());
}
```

The inputs to the **Equilateral** class are the number of classes and the normalized range. In the above code, there are three classes that are normalized
to the range -1 to 1, producing the following output:

```
0:  0.8660  ,   0.5000
1:-0.8660  ,   0.5000
2:  0.0000  ,  -1.0000
```

Notice that there are two outputs for each of the three classes. This decreases the number of neurons needed by one from the amount needed for one-of-n encoding. Equilateral encoding always requires one fewer output neuron than one-of-n encoding would have. Equilateral encoding is never used for fewer than three classes.

Look at the example before with equilateral normalization. Just as before, consider if the neural network had predicted a Versicolor iris, when it should have predicted a Verginica iris. The output and ideal are as follows:

```
Ideal  Output:    0.0000  ,  -1.0000
Actual Output:   -0.8660  ,   0.5000
```

In this case there are only two neurons, as is consistent with equilateral encoding. Now all neurons are producing incorrect values. Additionally, there are only two output neurons to process, slightly decreasing the complexity of the neural network.

Neural networks will rarely give output that exactly matches any of its training values. To deal with this in "one-of-n" encoding, look at which output neuron produced the highest output. This method does not work for equilateral encoding. Equilateral encoding shows which calculated class equilateral value (Listing 2.1) has the shortest distance to the actual output of the neural network.

What is meant by each of the sets being equal in distance from each other? It means that their Euclidean distance is equal. The Euclidean distance can be calculated using Equation 2.3.

$$d(\mathbf{p}, \mathbf{q}) = \sqrt{\sum_{i=1}^{n}(p_i - q_i)^2} \tag{2.5}$$

In the above equation the variable "q" represents the ideal output value; the variable "p" represents the actual output value. There are "n" sets of ideal and actual. Euclidean normalization is implemented using the **Equilateral** class in

Encog. Usually it is unnecessary to directly deal with the **Equilateral** class in Encog. Rather, one of the higher-level normalization methods described later in this chapter is used.

If you are interested in the precise means by which the equilateral numbers are calculated, visit the following URL:

http://www.heatonresearch.com/wiki/Equilateral

2.3 Programmatic Normalization

Encog provides a number of different means of normalizing data. The exact means that you use will be determined by exactly what you are trying to accomplish. The three methods for normalization are summarized here.

- Normalizing Individual Numbers

- Normalizing CSV Files

- Normalizing Memory Arrays

The next three sections will look at all three, beginning with normalizing individual numbers.

2.3.1 Normalizing Individual Numbers

Very often you will simply want to normalize or denormalize a single number. The range of values in your data is already known. For this case, it is unnecessary to go through the overhead of having Encog automatically discover ranges for you.

The "Lunar Lander" program is a good example of this. You can find the "Lunar Lander" example here.

```
org.encog.examples.neural.lunar.LunarLander
```

To perform the normalization, several **NormalizedField** objects are created. Here you see the **NormalizedField** object that was created for the lunar lander's fuel.

```
NormalizedField fuelStats =
    new NormalizedField(
      NormalizationAction.Normalize,
      "fuel",
      200,
      0,
      -0.9,
      0.9);
```

For the above example the range is normalized to -0.9 to 0.9. This is very similar to normalizing between -1 and 1, but less extreme. This can produce better results at times. It is also known that the acceptable range for fuel is between 0 and 200.

Now that the field object has been created, it is easy to normalize the values. Here the value 100 is normalized into the variable **n**.

```
double n = this.fuelStats.normalize(100);
```

To denormalize **n** back to the original fuel value, use the following code:

```
double f = this.fuelStats.denormalize(n);
```

Using the **NormalizedField** classes directly is useful when numbers arrive as the program runs. If large lists of numbers are already established, such as an array or CSV file, this method will not be as effective.

2.3.2   Normalizing Memory Arrays

To quickly normalize an array, the **NormalizeArray** class can be useful. This object works by normalizing one attribute at a time. An example of the normalize array class working is shown in the sunspot prediction example. This example can be found here:

```
org.encog.examples.neural.predict.sunspot.PredictSunspot
```

To begin, create an instance of the **NormalizeArray** object. Set the high and low range for normalization.

```
NormalizeArray  norm  =  new  NormalizeArray ( ) ;
norm . setNormalizedHigh (  1  ) ;
norm . setNormalizedLow (  −1  ) ;
```

Now raw data array can be normalized into a normalized array.

```
double [ ]  normalizedSunspots  =  norm . process ( rawDataArray ) ;
```

If you have an entire array to normalize to the same high/low, the **NormalizeArray** class works well. For more fine-tuned control, use the same techniques described in the previous section for individual values. However, all array elements must be looped over.

2.4   Normalizing CSV Files

If the data to be normalized is already stored in CSV files, Encog Analyst should be used to normalize the data. Encog Analyst can be used both through the Encog Workbench and directly from Java and C#. This section explains how to use it through Java to normalize the Iris data set.

To normalize a file, look at the file normalization example found at the following location:

```
org . encog . examples . neural . normalize . NormalizeFile
```

This example takes an input and output file. The input file is the iris data set. The first lines of this file are shown here:

```
"sepal_l" ," sepal_w" ," petal_l" ," petal_w" ," species "
5.1 ,3.5 ,1.4 ,0.2 , Iris −setosa
4.9 ,3.0 ,1.4 ,0.2 , Iris −setosa
4.7 ,3.2 ,1.3 ,0.2 , Iris −setosa
4.6 ,3.1 ,1.5 ,0.2 , Iris −setosa
5.0 ,3.6 ,1.4 ,0.2 , Iris −setosa
5.4 ,3.9 ,1.7 ,0.4 , Iris −setosa
4.6 ,3.4 ,1.4 ,0.3 , Iris −setosa
5.0 ,3.4 ,1.5 ,0.2 , Iris −setosa
```

The output will be a normalized version of the input file, as shown below:

```
"sepal_l","sepal_w","petal_l","petal_w","species(p0)","species(p1)
"
-0.55,0.24,-0.86,-0.91,-0.86,-0.5
-0.66,-0.16,-0.86,-0.91,-0.86,-0.5
-0.77,0,-0.89,-0.91,-0.86,-0.5
-0.83,-0.08,-0.83,-0.91,-0.86,-0.5
-0.61,0.33,-0.86,-0.91,-0.86,-0.5
-0.38,0.58,-0.76,-0.75,-0.86,-0.5
-0.83,0.16,-0.86,-0.83,-0.86,-0.5
-0.61,0.16,-0.83,-0.91,-0.86,-0.5
```

The above data shows that the numeric values have all been normalized to
between -1 and 1. Additionally, the species field is broken out into two parts.
This is because equilateral normalization was used on the species column.

2.4.1   Implementing Basic File Normalization

In the last section, you saw how Encog Analyst normalizes a file. In this
section, you will learn the programming code necessary to accomplish this.
Begin by accessing the source and target files:

```
File  sourceFile = new File(args[0]);
File  targetFile = new File(args[1]);
```

Now create instances of **EncogAnalyst** and **AnalystWizard**. The wizard
will analyze the source file and build all of the normalization stats needed to
perform the normalization.

```
EncogAnalyst analyst = new EncogAnalyst();
AnalystWizard wizard = new AnalystWizard(analyst);
```

The wizard can now be started.

```
wizard.wizard(sourceFile, true, AnalystFileFormat.DECPNT_COMMA);
```

Now that the input file has been analyzed, it is time to create a normalization
object. This object will perform the actual normalization.

```
final AnalystNormalizeCSV norm = new AnalystNormalizeCSV();
norm.analyze(sourceFile, true, CSVFormat.ENGLISH, analyst);
```

It is necessary to specify the output format for the CSV, in this case, use ENGLISH, which specifies a decimal point. It is also important to produce output headers to easily identify all attributes.

```
norm.setOutputFormat(CSVFormat.ENGLISH);
norm.setProduceOutputHeaders(true);
```

Finally, we normalize the file.

```
norm.normalize(targetFile);
```

Now that the data is normalized, the normalization stats may be saved for later use. This is covered in the next section.

2.4.2   Saving the Normalization Script

Encog keeps statistics on normalized data. This data, called the normalization stats, tells Encog the numeric ranges for each attribute that was normalized. This data can be saved so that it does not need to be renormalized each time.

To save a stats file, use the following command:

```
analyst.save(new File("stats.ega"));
```

The file can be later reloaded with the following command:

```
analyst.load(new File("stats.ega"));
```

The extension EGA is common and stands for "Encog Analyst."

2.4.3   Customizing File Normalization

The Encog Analyst contains a collection of **AnalystField** objects. These objects hold the type of normalization and the ranges of each attribute. This collection can be directly accessed to change how the attributes are normalized. Also, **AnalystField** objects can be removed and excludes from the final output.

The following code shows how to access each of the fields determined by the wizard.

```
System.out.println("Fields found in file :");
for (AnalystField field : analyst.getScript().getNormalize()
.getNormalizedFields()) {
  StringBuilder line = new StringBuilder();
  line.append(field.getName());
  line.append(",action=");
  line.append(field.getAction());
  line.append(",min=");
  line.append(field.getActualLow());
  line.append(",max=");
  line.append(field.getActualHigh());
  System.out.println(line.toString());
}
```

There are several important attributes on each of the **AnalystField** objects.
For example, to change the normalization range to 0 to 1, execute the following
commands:

```
field.setNormalizedHigh(1);
field.setNormalizedLow(0);
```

The mode of normalization can also be changed. To use one-of-n normalization
instead of equilateral, just use the following command:

```
field.setAction(NormalizationAction.OneOf);
```

Encog Analyst can do much more than just normalize data. It is also performs
the entire normalization, training and evaluation of a neural network. This
will be covered in greater detail in Chapters 3 and 4. Chapter 3 will show how
to do this from the workbench, while Chapter 4 will show how to do this from
code.

2.5   Summary

This chapter explained how to obtain and normalize data for Encog. There are
many different sources of data. One of the best is the UCI Machine Learning
Repository, which provides many of the dataset examples in this book.

There are two broad classes of data to normalize: numeric and non-numeric
data. These two data classes each have techniques for normalization.

Numeric data is normalized by mapping values to a specific range, often from -1 to +1. Another common range is between 0 and +1. Formulas were provided earlier in this chapter for both normalization and denormalization.

Non-numeric data is usually an attribute that defines a class. For the case of the iris dataset, the iris species is a non-numeric class. To normalize these classes, they must be converted to an array of floating point values, just as with numeric data.

Encog supports two types of nominal normalization. The first is called "one-of-n." One-of-n creates a number of neurons equal to the number of class items. The class number to be encoded is given a value of 1. Others are given zeros.

Equilateral encoding is another way to encode a class. For equilateral encoding, a number of neurons is used that equals one, less the number of class items. A code of floating point numbers is created for each class item with uniform equilateral distance to the other class data items. This allows all output neurons to play a part in each class item and causes an error to affect more neurons than one-of-n encoding.

This chapter introduced the Encog Analyst and explained its use to normalize data. The Encog Analyst can also be used in the Encog Workbench. The Encog Workbench is a GUI application that allows many of the features of neural networks to be accessed without the need to write code.

Chapter 3

The Encog Workbench

- Structure of the Encog Workbench

- A Simple XOR Example

- Using the Encog Analyst

- Encog Analyst Reports

The Encog Workbench is a GUI application that enables many different machine learning tasks without writing Java or C# code. The Encog Workbench itself is written in Java, but generates files that can be used with any Encog framework.

The Encog Workbench is distributed as a single self-executing JAR file. On most operating systems, the Encog Workbench JAR file is started simply by double-clicking. This includes Microsoft Windows, Macintosh and some variants of Linux. To start from the command line, the following command is used.

```
java −jar ./encog−workbench−3.0.0−executable
```

Depending on the version of Encog, the above JAR file might have a different name. No matter the version, the file will have "encog-workbench" and "executable" somewhere in its name. No other JAR files are necessary for the workbench as all third-party JAR files were are placed inside this JAR.

3.1   Structure of the Encog Workbench

Before studying how the Encog Workbench is actually used, we will learn
about its structure. The workbench works with a project directory that holds
all of the files needed for a project. The Encog Workbench project contains
no subdirectories. Also, if a subdirectory is added into an Encog Workbench
project, it simply becomes another independent project.

There is also no main "project file" inside an Encog Workbench project.
Often a readme.txt or readme.html file is placed inside of an Encog Workbench
project to explain what to do with the project. However, this file is included
at the discretion of the project creator.

There are several different file types that might be placed in an Encog
workbench project. These files are organized by their file extension. The
extension of a file is how the Encog Workbench knows what to do with that
file. The following extensions are recognized by the Encog Workbench:

- .csv

- .eg

- .ega

- .egb

- .gif

- .html

- .jpg

- .png

- .txt

The following sections will discuss the purpose of each file type.

3.1.1   Workbench CSV Files

An acronym for "comma separated values," CSV files hold tabular data. However, CSV files are not always "comma separated." This is especially true in parts of the world that use a decimal comma instead of a decimal point. The CSV files used by Encog can be based on a decimal comma. In this case, a semicolon (;) should be used as the field separator.

CSV files may also have headers to define what each column of the CSV file means. Column headers are optional, but very much suggested. Column headers name the attributes and provide consistency across the both the CSV files created by Encog and provided by the user.

A CSV file defines the data used by Encog. Each row in the CSV file defines a training set element and each column defines an attribute. If a particular attribute is not known for a training set element, then the "?" character should be placed in that row/column. Encog deals with missing values in various ways. This is discussed later in this chapter in the Encog analyst discussion.

A CSV file cannot be used to directly train a neural network, but must first be converted into an EGB file. To convert a CSV file to an EGB file, right-click the CSV file and choose "Export to Training (EGB)." EGB files nicely define what columns are input and ideal data, while CSV files do not offer any distinction. Rather, CSV files might represent raw data provided by the user. Additionally, some CSV files are generated by Encog as raw user data is processed.

3.1.2   Workbench EG Files

Encog EG files store a variety of different object types, but in themselves are simply text files. All data inside of EG files is stored with decimal points and comma separator, regardless of the geographic region in which Encog is running. While CSV files can be formatted according to local number formatting rules, EG files cannot. This is to keep EG files consistent across all Encog platforms.

The following object types are stored in EG files.

- Machine Learning Methods (i.e. Neural Networks)

- NEAT Populations

- Training Continuation Data

The Encog workbench will display the object type of any EG file that is located in the project directory. An Encog EG file only stores one object per file. If multiple objects are to be stored, they must be stored in separate EG files.

3.1.3   Workbench EGA Files

Encog Analyst script files, or EGA files, hold instructions for the Encog analyst. These files hold statistical information about what a CSV file is designed to analyze. EGA files also hold script information that describes how to process raw data. EGA files are executable by the workbench.

A full discussion of the EGA file and every possible configuration/script item is beyond the scope of this book. However, a future book will be dedicated to the Encog Analyst. Additional reference information about the Encog Analyst script file can be found here:

http://www.heatonresearch.com/wiki/EGA_File

Later in this chapter, we will create an EGA file to analyze the iris dataset.

3.1.4   Workbench EGB Files

Encog binary files, or EGB files, hold training data. As previously discussed, CSV files are typically converted to EGB for Encog. This data is stored in a platform-independent binary format. Because of this, EGB files are read much faster than a CSV file. Additionally, the EGB file internally contains the number of input and ideal columns present in the file. CSV files must be converted to EGB files prior to training. To convert a CSV file to an EGB file, right-click the selected CSV file and choose "Export to Training (EGB)."

3.1.5   Workbench Image Files

The Encog workbench does not directly work with image files at this point, but can be displayed by double-clicking. The Encog workbench is capable of displaying PNG, JPG and GIF files.

3.1.6   Workbench Text Files

Encog Workbench does not directly use text files. However, text files are a means of storing instructions for project file users. For instance, a readme.txt file can be added to a project and displayed inside of the analyst. The Encog Workbench can display both text and HTML files.

3.2   A Simple XOR Example

There are many different ways that the Encog Workbench can be used. The Encog Analyst can be used to create projects that include normalization, training and analysis. However, all of the individual neural network parts can also manually created and trained. If the data is already normalized, Encog Analyst may not be necessary.

In this section we will see how to use the Encog Workbench without the Encog Analyst by creating a simple XOR neural network. The XOR dataset does not require any normalization as itis already in the 0 to 1 range.

We will begin by creating a new project.

3.2.1   Creating a New Project

First create a new project by launching the Encog Workbench. Once the Encog Workbench starts up, the options of creating a new project, opening an existing project or quitting will appear. Choose to create a new project and name it "XOR." This will create a new empty folder named XOR. You will now see the Encog Workbench in Figure 3.1.

Figure 3.1: The Encog Workbench

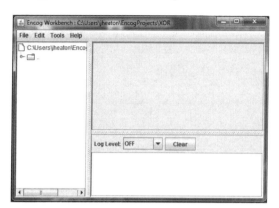

This is the basic layout of the Encog Workbench. There are three main areas. The tall rectangle on the left is where all project files are shown. Currently this project has no files. You can also see the log output and status information. The rectangle just above the log output is where documents are opened. The look of the Encog Workbench is very much like IDE and should be familiar to developers.

3.2.2   Generate Training Data

The next step is to obtain training data. There are several ways to do this. First, Encog Workbench supports drag and drop. For instance, CSVs can be dragged from the operating system and dropped into the project as a copy, leaving the original file unchanged. These files will then appear in the project tree.

The Encog Workbench comes with a number of built-in training sets. Additionally, it can download external data such as stock prices and even sunspot information. The sunspot information can be used for time-series prediction experiments.

The Encog Workbench also has a built-in XOR training set. To access it, choose Tools->Generate Training Data. This will open the "Create Training Data" dialog. Choose "XOR Training Set" and name it "xor.csv." Your new CSV file will appear in the project tree.

If you double-click the "xor.csv" file, you will see the following training data in Listing 3.1:

Listing 3.1: XOR Training Data

```
"op1","op2","result"
0,0,0
1,0,1
0,1,1
1,1,0
```

It is important to note that the file does have headers. This must be specified when the EGB file is generated.

3.2.3   Create a Neural Network

Now that the training data has been created, a neural network should be created learn the XOR data. To create a neural network, choose "File->New File." Then choose "Machine Learning Method" and name the neural network "xor.eg." Choose "Feedforward Neural Network." This will display the dialog shown in Figure 3.2:

Figure 3.2: Create a Feedforward Network

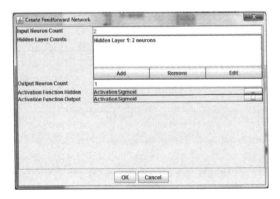

Make sure to fill in the dialog exactly as above. There should be two input neurons, one output neuron and a single hidden layer with two neurons. Choose both activation functions to be sigmoid. Once the neural network is created, it will appear on the project tree.

3.2.4   Train the Neural Network

It is now time to train the neural network. The neural network that you see currently is untrained. To easily determine if the neural network is untrained, double-click the EG file that contains the neural network. This will show Figure 3.3.

Figure 3.3: Editing the Network

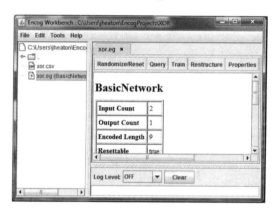

This screen shows some basic stats on the neural network. To see more detail, select the "Visualize" button and choose "Network Structure." This will show Figure 3.4.

Figure 3.4: Network Structure

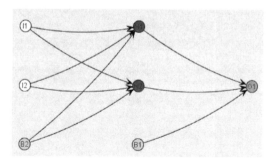

The input and output neurons are shown from the structure view. All of the connections between with the hidden layer and bias neurons are also visible. The bias neurons, as well as the hidden layer, help the neural network to learn.

With this complete, it is time to actually train the neural network. Begin by closing the histogram visualization and the neural network. There should be no documents open inside of the workbench.

Right-click the "xor.csv" training data. Choose "Export to Training (EGB)." Fill in two input neurons and one output neuron on the dialog that appears. On the next dialog, be sure to specify that there are headers. Once this is complete, an EGB file will be added to the project tree. This will result in three files: an EG file, an EGB file and a CSV file.

To train the neural network, choose "Tools->Train." This will open a dialog to choose the training set and machine learning method. Because there is only one EG file and one EGB file, this dialog should default to the correct values. Leave the "Load to Memory" checkbox clicked. As this is such a small training set, there is no reason to not load to memory.

There are many different training methods to choose from. For this example, choose "Propagation - Resilient." Accept all default parameters for this training type. Once this is complete, the training progress tab will appear. Click "Start" to begin training.

Training will usually finish in under a second. However, if the training continues for several seconds, the training may need to be reset by clicking the drop list titled "<Select Option>." Choose to reset the network. Because a neural network starts with random weights, training times will vary. On a small neural network such as XOR, the weights can potentially be bad enough that the network never trains. If this is the case, simply reset the network as it trains.

3.2.5 Evaluate the Neural Network

There are two ways to evaluate the neural network. The first is to simply calculate the neural network error by choosing "Tools->Evaluate Network." You will be prompted for the machine learning method and training data to use. This will show you the neural network error when evaluated against the specified training set.

For this example, the error will be a percent. When evaluating this percent, the lower the percent the better. Other machine learning methods may generate an error as a number or other value.

For a more advanced evaluation, choose "Tools->Validation Chart." This will result in an output similar to Figure 3.5.

Figure 3.5: Validation Chart for XOR

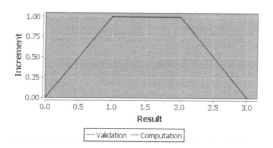

This graphically depicts how close the neural network's computation matches the ideal value (validation). As shown in this example, they are extremely close.

3.3   Using the Encog Analyst

In the last section we used the Workbench with a simple data set that did not need normalization. In this section we will use the Encog Analyst to work with a more complex data set - the iris data set that has already been demonstrated several times. The normalization procedure is already explored. However, this will provide an example of how to normalize and produce a neural network for it using the Encog Analyst

The iris dataset is built into the Encog Workbench, so it is easy to create a dataset for it. Create a new Encog Workbench project as described in the previous section. Name this new project "Iris." To obtain the iris data set, choose "Tools->Generate Training Data." Choose the "Iris Dataset" and name it "iris.csv."

Right-click the "iris.csv" file and choose "Analyst Wizard." This will bring up a dialog like Figure 3.6.

Figure 3.6: Encog Analyst Wizard

You can accept most default values. However, "Target Field" and "CSV File Headers" fields should be changed. Specify "species" as the target and indicate that there are headers. The other two tabs should remain unchanged. Click "OK" and the wizard will generate an EGA file.

This exercise also gave the option to show how to deal with missing values. While the iris dataset has no missing values, this is not the case with every dataset. The default action is to discard them. However, you can also choose to average them out.

Double click this EGA file to see its contents as in Figure 3.7.

Figure 3.7: Edit an EGA File

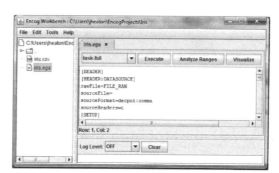

From this tab you can execute the EGA file. Click "Execute" and a status dialog will be displayed. From here, click "Start" to begin the process. The entire execution should take under a minute on most computers.

- Step 1: Randomize - Shuffle the file into a random order.

- Step 2: Segregate - Create a training data set and an evaluation data set.

- Step 3: Normalize - Normalize the data into a form usable by the selected Machine Learning Method

- Step 4: Generate - Generate the training data into an EGB file that can be used to train.

- Step 5: Create - Generate the selected Machine Learning Method.

- Step 6: Train - Train the selected Machine Learning Method.

- Step 7: Evaluate - Evaluate the Machine Learning Method.

This process will also create a number of files. The complete list of files, in this project is:

- iris.csv - The raw data.

- iris.ega - The EGA file. This is the Encog Analyst script.

- iris_eval.csv - The evaluation data.

- iris_norm.csv - The normalized version of iris_train.csv.

- iris_output.csv - The output from running iris_eval.csv.

- iris_random.csv - The randomized output from running iris.csv.

- iris_train.csv - The training data.

- iris_train.eg - The Machine Learning Method that was trained.

- iris_train.egb - The binary training data, created from iris_norm.egb.

If you change the EGA script file or use different options for the wizard, you may have different steps.

To see how the network performed, open the iris_output.csv file. You will see Listing 3.2.

Listing 3.2: Evaluation of the Iris Data

```
"sepal_l","sepal_w","petal_l","petal_w","species","Output:species"
6.5,3.0,5.8,2.2,Iris−virginica,Iris−virginica
6.2,3.4,5.4,2.3,Iris−virginica,Iris−virginica
7.7,3.0,6.1,2.3,Iris−virginica,Iris−virginica
6.8,3.0,5.5,2.1,Iris−virginica,Iris−virginica
6.5,3.0,5.5,1.8,Iris−virginica,Iris−virginica
6.3,3.3,4.7,1.6,Iris−versicolor,Iris−versicolor
5.6,2.9,3.6,1.3,Iris−versicolor,Iris−versicolor
...
```

This illustrates how the neural network attempts to predict what iris species each row belongs to. As you can see, it is correct for all of the rows shown here. These are data items that the neural network was not originally trained with.

3.4 Encog Analyst Reports

This section will discuss how the Encog Workbench can also produce several Encog Analyst reports. To produce these reports, open the EGA file as seen in Figure 3.7. Clicking the "Visualize" button gives you several visualization options. Choose either a "Range Report" or "Scatter Plot." Both of these are discussed in the next sections.

3.4.1 Range Report

The range report shows the ranges of each of the attributes that are used to perform normalization by the Encog Analyst. Figure 3.8 shows the beginning of the range report.

Figure 3.8: Encog Analyst Range Report

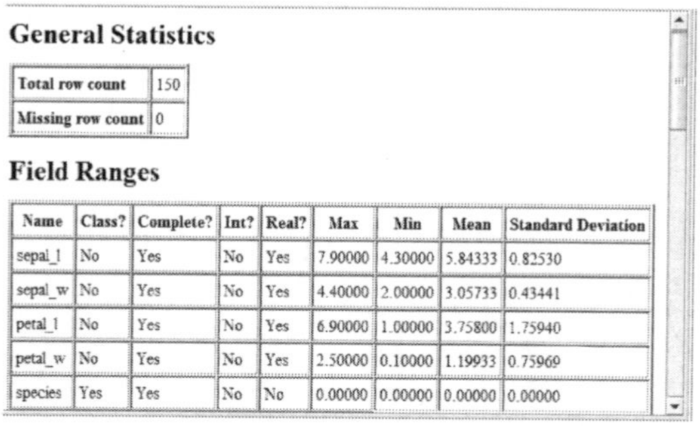

General Statistics

Total row count	150
Missing row count	0

Field Ranges

Name	Class?	Complete?	Int?	Real?	Max	Min	Mean	Standard Deviation
sepal_l	No	Yes	No	Yes	7.90000	4.30000	5.84333	0.82530
sepal_w	No	Yes	No	Yes	4.40000	2.00000	3.05733	0.43441
petal_l	No	Yes	No	Yes	6.90000	1.00000	3.75800	1.75940
petal_w	No	Yes	No	Yes	2.50000	0.10000	1.19933	0.75969
species	Yes	Yes	No	No	0.00000	0.00000	0.00000	0.00000

This is only the top portion. Additional information is available by scrolling down.

3.4.2 Scatter Plot

It is also possible to display a scatter plot to view the relationship between two or more attributes. When choosing to display a scatter plot, Encog Analyst will prompt you to choose which attributes to relate. If you choose just two, you are shown a regular scatter plot. If you choose all four, you will be shown a multivariate scatter plot as seen in Figure 3.9.

Figure 3.9: Encog Analyst Multivariate Scatter Plot Report

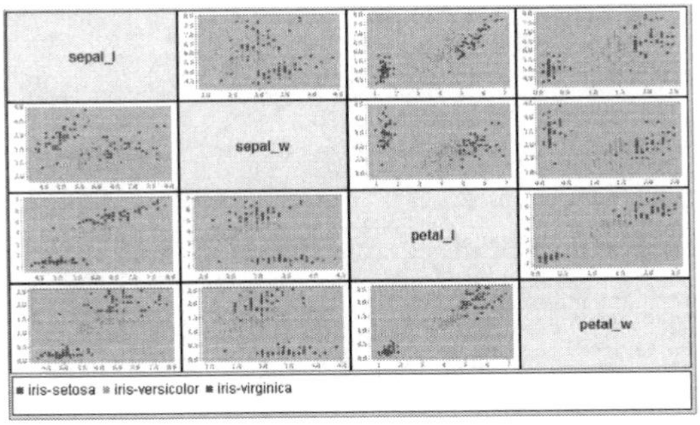

This illustrates how four variables relate. To see how to variables relate, choose two squares on the diagonal. Follow the row and column on each and the square that intersects is the relationship between those two attributes. It is also important to note that the triangle formed above the diagonal is the mirror image (reverse) of the triangle below the diagonal.

3.5   Summary

This chapter introduced the Encog Workbench. The Encog Workbench is a GUI application that visually works with neural networks and other machine learning methods. The workbench is a Java application that produces data that it works across any Encog platforms.

This chapter also demonstrated how to use Encog Workbench to directly create and train a neural network. For cases where data is already normalized, this is a good way to train and evaluate neural networks. The workbench creates and trains neural networks to accomplish this.

For more complex data, Encog Analyst is a valuable tool that performs automatic normalization. It also organizes a neural network project as a series of tasks to be executed. The iris dataset was used to illustrate how to use the Encog Analyst.

So far, this book has shown how to normalize and process data using the Encog Analyst. The next chapter shows how to construct neural networks with code using the Encog framework directly with and without Encog Analyst.

Chapter 4

Constructing Neural Networks in Java

- Constructing a Neural Network

- Activation Functions

- Encog Persistence

- Using the Encog Analyst from Code

This chapter will show how to construct feedforward and simple recurrent neural networks with Encog and how to save these neural networks for later use. Both of these neural network types are created using the **BasicNetwork** and **BasicLayer** classes. In addition to these two classes, activation functions are also used. The role of activation functions will be discussed as well.

Neural networks can take a considerable amount of time to train. Because of this it is important to save your neural networks. Encog neural networks can be persisted using Java's built-in serialization. This persistence can also be achieved by writing the neural network to an EG file, a cross-platform text file. This chapter will introduce both forms of persistence.

In the last chapter, the Encog Analyst was used to automatically normalize data. The Encog Analyst can also automatically create neural networks based on CSV data. This chapter will show how to use the Encog analyst to create neural networks from code.

4.1   Constructing a Neural Network

A simple neural network can quickly be created using **BasicLayer** and **BasicNetwork** objects. The following code creates several **BasicLayer** objects with a default hyperbolic tangent activation function.

```
BasicNetwork network = new BasicNetwork();
network.addLayer(new BasicLayer(2));
network.addLayer(new BasicLayer(3));
network.addLayer(new BasicLayer(1));
network.getStructure().finalizeStructure();
network.reset();
```

This network will have an input layer of two neurons, a hidden layer with three neurons and an output layer with a single neuron. To use an activation function other than the hyperbolic tangent function, use code similar to the following:

```
BasicNetwork network = new BasicNetwork();
network.addLayer(new BasicLayer(null,true,2));
network.addLayer(new BasicLayer(new ActivationSigmoid(),true,3));
network.addLayer(new BasicLayer(new ActivationSigmoid(),false,1));
network.getStructure().finalizeStructure();
network.reset();
```

The sigmoid activation function is passed to the **AddLayer** calls for the hidden and output layer. The **true** value that was also introduced specifies that the **BasicLayer** should have a bias neuron. The output layer does not have bias neurons, and the input layer does not have an activation function. This is because the bias neuron affects the next layer, and the activation function affects data coming from the previous layer.

Unless Encog is being used for something very experimental, always use a bias neuron. Bias neurons allow the activation function to shift off the origin of zero. This allows the neural network to produce a zero value even when the inputs are not zero. The following URL provides a more mathematical justification for the importance of bias neurons:

http://www.heatonresearch.com/wiki/Bias

Activation functions are attached to layers and used to scale data output from a layer. Encog applies a layer's activation function to the data that the layer is about to output. If an activation function is not specified for **BasicLayer**, the hyperbolic tangent activation will be defaulted.

It is also possible to create context layers. A context layer can be used to create an Elman or Jordan style neural networks. The following code could be used to create an Elman neural network.

```
BasicLayer input, hidden;
BasicNetwork network = new BasicNetwork();
network.addLayer(input = new BasicLayer(1));
network.addLayer(hidden = new BasicLayer(2));
network.addLayer(new BasicLayer(1));
input.setContextFedBy(hidden);
network.getStructure().finalizeStructure();
network.reset();
```

Notice the **hidden.setContextFedBy** line? This creates a context link from the output layer to the hidden layer. The hidden layer will always be fed the output from the last iteration. This creates an Elman style neural network. Elman and Jordan networks will be introduced in Chapter 7.

4.2   The Role of Activation Functions

The last section illustrated how to assign activation functions to layers. Activation functions are used by many neural network architectures to scale the output from layers. Encog provides many different activation functions that can be used to construct neural networks. The next sections will introduce these activation functions.

Activation functions are attached to layers and are used to scale data output from a layer. Encog applies a layer's activation function to the data that the layer is about to output. If an activation function is not specified for **BasicLayer**, the hyperbolic tangent activation will be the defaulted. All classes that serve as activation functions must implement the **ActivationFunction** interface.

Activation functions play a very important role in training neural networks.

Propagation training, which will be covered in the next chapter, requires than an activation function have a valid derivative. Not all activation functions have valid derivatives. Determining if an activation function has a derivative may be an important factor in choosing an activation function.

4.3   Encog Activation Functions

The next sections will explain each of the activation functions supported by Encog. There are several factors to consider when choosing an activation function. Firstly, it is important to consider how the type of neural network being used dictates the activation function required. Secondly, consider the necessity of training the neural network using propagation. Propagation training requires an activation function that provides a derivative. Finally, consider the range of numbers to be used. Some activation functions deal with only positive numbers or numbers in a particular range.

4.3.1   ActivationBiPolar

The **ActivationBiPolar** activation function is used with neural networks that require bipolar values. Bipolar values are either **true** or **false**. A **true** value is represented by a bipolar value of 1; a **false** value is represented by a bipolar value of -1. The bipolar activation function ensures that any numbers passed to it are either -1 or 1. The **ActivationBiPolar** function does this with the following code:

```
if (d[i] > 0) {
   d[i] = 1;
} else {
   d[i] = -1;
}
```

As shown above, the output from this activation is limited to either -1 or 1. This sort of activation function is used with neural networks that require bipolar output from one layer to the next. There is no derivative function for bipolar, so this activation function cannot be used with propagation training.

4.3.2   Activation Competitive

The **ActivationCompetitive** function is used to force only a select group of neurons to win. The winner is the group of neurons with the highest output. The outputs of each of these neurons are held in the array passed to this function. The size of the winning neuron group is definable. The function will first determine the winners. All non-winning neurons will be set to zero. The winners will all have the same value, which is an even division of the sum of the winning outputs.

This function begins by creating an array that will track whether each neuron has already been selected as one of the winners. The number of winners is also counted.

```
final boolean [] winners = new boolean[x.length];
double sumWinners = 0;
```

First, loop **maxWinners** a number of times to find that number of winners.

```
// find the desired number of winners
for (int i = 0; i < this.params[0]; i++) {
  double maxFound = Double.NEGATIVE_INFINITY;
  int winner = -1;
```

Now, one winner must be determined. Loop over all of the neuron outputs and find the one with the highest output.

```
  for (int j = start; j < start + size; j++) {
```

If this neuron has not already won and it has the maximum output, it might be a winner if no other neuron has a higher activation.

```
    if (!winners[j] && (x[j] > maxFound)) {
      winner = j;
      maxFound = x[j];
    }
  }
```

Keep the sum of the winners that were found and mark this neuron as a winner. Marking it a winner will prevent it from being chosen again. The sum of the winning outputs will ultimately be divided among the winners.

```
    sumWinners += maxFound;
    winners[winner] = true;
}
```

Now that the correct number of winners is determined, the values must be adjusted for winners and non-winners. The non-winners will all be set to zero. The winners will share the sum of the values held by all winners.

```
// adjust weights for winners and non-winners
for (int i = start; i < start + size; i++) {
  if (winners[i]) {
    x[i] = x[i] / sumWinners;
  } else {
    x[i] = 0.0;
  }
}
```

This sort of an activation function can be used with competitive, learning neural networks such as the self-organizing map. This activation function has no derivative, so it cannot be used with propagation training.

4.3.3   ActivationLinear

The **ActivationLinear** function is really no activation function at all. It simply implements the linear function. The linear function can be seen in Equation 4.1.

$$f(x) = x \tag{4.1}$$

The graph of the linear function is a simple line, as seen in Figure 4.1.

Figure 4.1: Graph of the Linear Activation Function

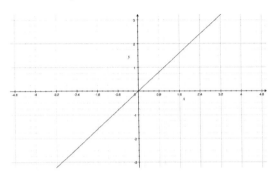

The Java implementation for the linear activation function is very simple. It does nothing. The input is returned as it was passed.

```
public final void activationFunction(final double[] x, final int
    start,
final int size) {
}
```

The linear function is used primarily for specific types of neural networks that have no activation function, such as the self-organizing map. The linear activation function has a constant derivative of one, so it can be used with propagation training. Linear layers are sometimes used by the output layer of a propagation-trained feedforward neural network.

4.3.4 ActivationLOG

The **ActivationLog** activation function uses an algorithm based on the log function. The following shows how this activation function is calculated.

$$f(x) = \begin{cases} \log(1+x) & , x >= 0 \\ \log(1-x) & , \text{otherwise} \end{cases} \tag{4.2}$$

This produces a curve similar to the hyperbolic tangent activation function, which will be discussed later in this chapter. The graph for the logarithmic activation function is shown in Figure 4.2.

Figure 4.2: Graph of the Logarithmic Activation Function

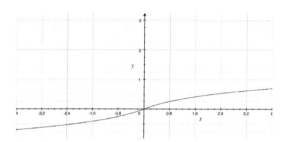

The logarithmic activation function can be useful to prevent saturation. A hidden node of a neural network is considered saturated when, on a given set of inputs, the output is approximately 1 or -1 in most cases. This can slow training significantly. This makes the logarithmic activation function a possible choice when training is not successful using the hyperbolic tangent activation function.

As illustrated in Figure 4.2, the logarithmic activation function spans both positive and negative numbers. This means it can be used with neural networks where negative number output is desired. Some activation functions, such as the sigmoid activation function will only produce positive output. The logarithmic activation function does have a derivative, so it can be used with propagation training.

4.3.5   ActivationSigmoid

The **ActivationSigmoid** activation function should only be used when positive number output is expected because the **ActivationSigmoid** function will only produce positive output. The equation for the **ActivationSigmoid** function can be seen in Equation 4.2.

$$f(x) = \frac{1}{1 + e^{-x}} \tag{4.3}$$

The **ActivationSigmoid** function will move negative numbers into the positive range. This can be seen in Figure 4.3, which shows the graph of the sigmoid function.

Figure 4.3: Graph of the ActivationSigmoid Function

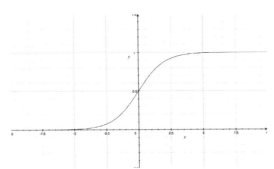

The **ActivationSigmoid** function is a very common choice for feedforward and simple recurrent neural networks. However, it is imperative that the training data does not expect negative output numbers. If negative numbers are required, the hyperbolic tangent activation function may be a better solution.

4.3.6 ActivationSoftMax

The **ActivationSoftMax** activation function will scale all of the input values so that the sum will equal one. The **ActivationSoftMax** activation function is sometimes used as a hidden layer activation function.

The activation function begins by summing the natural exponent of all of the neuron outputs.

```
double sum = 0;
for (int i = 0; i < d.length; i++) {
  d[i] = BoundMath.exp(d[i]);
  sum += d[i];
}
```

The output from each of the neurons is then scaled according to this sum. This produces outputs that will sum to 1.

```
for (int i = start; i < start + size; i++) {
  x[i] = x[i] / sum;
}
```

The **ActivationSoftMax** is typically used in the output layer of a neural network for classification.

4.3.7 ActivationTANH

The **ActivationTANH** activation function uses the hyperbolic tangent function. The hyperbolic tangent activation function is probably the most commonly used activation function as it works with both negative and positive numbers. The hyperbolic tangent function is the default activation function for Encog. The equation for the hyperbolic tangent activation function can be seen in Equation 4.3.

$$f(x) = \frac{e^{2x} - 1}{e^{2x} + 1} \tag{4.4}$$

The fact that the hyperbolic tangent activation function accepts both positive and negative numbers can be seen in Figure 4.4, which shows the graph of the hyperbolic tangent function.

Figure 4.4: Graph of the Hyperbolic Tangent Activation Function

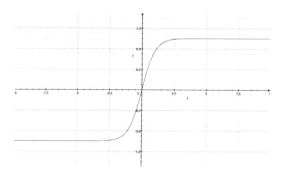

The hyperbolic tangent function is a very common choice for feedforward and simple recurrent neural networks. The hyperbolic tangent function has a derivative so it can be used with propagation training.

4.4   Encog Persistence

It can take considerable time to train a neural network and it is important
to take measures to guarantee your work is saved once the network has been
trained. Encog provides several means for this data to be saved, with two
primary ways to store Encog data objects. Encog offers file-based persistence
or Java's own persistence.

Java provides its own means to serialize objects and is called Java serialization. Java serialization allows many different object types to be written to a
stream, such as a disk file. Java serialization for Encog works the same way as
with any Java object using Java serialization. Every important Encog object
that should support serialization implements the **Serializable** interface.

Java serialization is a quick way to store an Encog object. However, it
has some important limitations. The files created with Java serialization can
only be used by Encog for Java; they will be incompatible with Encog for
.Net or Encog for Silverlight. Further, Java serialization is directly tied to
the underlying objects. As a result, future versions of Encog may not be
compatible with your serialized files.

To create universal files that will work with all Encog platforms, consider
the Encog EG format. The EG format stores neural networks as flat text files
ending in the extension .EG.

This chapter will introduce both methods of Encog persistence, beginning
with Encog EG persistence. The chapter will end by exploring how a neural
network is saved in an Encog persistence file.

4.5   Using Encog EG Persistence

Encog EG persistence files are the native file format for Encog and are stored
with the extension .EG. The Encog Workbench uses the Encog EG to process
files. This format can be exchanged over different operating systems and Encog
platforms, making it the choice format choice for an Encog application.

This section begins by looking at an XOR example that makes use of
Encog's EG files. Later, this same example will be used for Java serialization.

We will begin with the Encog EG persistence example.

4.5.1   Using Encog EG Persistence

Encog EG persistence is very easy to use. The **EncogDirectoryPersistence** class is used to load and save objects from an Encog EG file. The following is a good example of Encog EG persistence:

```
org.encog.examples.neural.persist.EncogPersistence
```

This example is made up of two primary methods. The first method, **trainAnd-Save**, trains a neural network and then saves it to an Encog EG file. The second method, **loadAndEvaluate,** loads the Encog EG file and evaluates it. This proves that the Encog EG file was saved correctly. The **main** method simply calls these two in sequence. We will begin by examining the **trainAnd-Save** method.

```java
public void trainAndSave() {
  System.out.println(
    "Training XOR network to under 1% error rate.");
```

This method begins by creating a basic neural network to be trained with the XOR operator. It is a simple three-layer feedforward neural network.

```java
BasicNetwork network = new BasicNetwork();
network.addLayer(new BasicLayer(2));
network.addLayer(new BasicLayer(6));
network.addLayer(new BasicLayer(1));
network.getStructure().finalizeStructure();
network.reset();
```

A training set is created that contains the expected outputs and inputs for the XOR operator.

```java
MLDataSet trainingSet =
  new BasicMLDataSet(XOR_INPUT, XOR_IDEAL);
```

This neural network will be trained using resilient propagation (RPROP).

```java
// train the neural network
final MLTrain train =
  new ResilientPropagation(network, trainingSet);
```

RPROP iterations are performed until the error rate is very small. Training will be covered in the next chapter. For now, training is a means to verify that the error remains the same after a network reload.

```
do {
    train.iteration();
} while(train.getError() > 0.009);
```

Once the network has been trained, display the final error rate. The neural network can now be saved.

```
double e = network.calculateError(trainingSet);
System.out.println("Network traiined to error: "
+ e);
System.out.println("Saving network");
```

The network can now be saved to a file. Only one Encog object is saved per file. This is done using the **saveObject** method of the **EncogDirectoryPersistence** class.

```
System.out.println("Saving network");
EncogDirectoryPersistence.saveObject(new File(FILENAME), network);
```

Now that the Encog EG file has been created, load the neural network back from the file to ensure it still performs well using the **loadAndEvaluate** method.

```
public void loadAndEvaluate()
{
    System.out.println("Loading network");
    BasicNetwork network =
      (BasicNetwork)EncogDirectoryPersistence.loadObject(
      new File(FILENAME));
```

Now that the collection has been constructed, load the network named **network** that was saved earlier. It is important to evaluate the neural network to prove that it is still trained. To do this, create a training set for the XOR operator.

```
MLDataSet trainingSet =
    new BasicMLDataSet(XOR_INPUT, XOR_IDEAL);
```

Calculate the error for the given training data.

```
  double e = network.calculateError(trainingSet);
  System.out.println(
    "Loaded network's error is(should be same as above): " + e);
}
```

This error is displayed and should be the same as before the network was saved.

4.6   Using Java Serialization

It is also possible to use standard Java serialization with Encog neural networks and training sets. Encog EG persistence is much more flexible than Java serialization. However, there are cases a neural network can simply be saved to a platform-dependant binary file. This example shows how to use Java serialization with Encog. The example begins by calling the **trainAndSave** method.

```
public void trainAndSave() throws IOException {
  System.out.println(
    "Training XOR network to under 1% error rate.");
```

This method begins by creating a basic neural network to be trained with the XOR operator. It is a simple, three-layer feedforward neural network.

```
  BasicNetwork network = new BasicNetwork();
  network.addLayer(new BasicLayer(2));
  network.addLayer(new BasicLayer(6));
  network.addLayer(new BasicLayer(1));
  network.getStructure().finalizeStructure();
  network.reset();
  MLDataSet trainingSet =
    new BasicMLDataSet(XOR_INPUT, XOR_IDEAL);
```

We will train this neural network using resilient propagation (RPROP).

```
  // train the neural network
  final MLTrain train =
    new ResilientPropagation(network, trainingSet);
```

The following code loops through training iterations until the error rate is below one percent (<0.01).

```
do {
   train.iteration();
} while(train.getError() > 0.01);
```

The final error for the neural network is displayed.

```
double e = network.calculateError(trainingSet);
System.out.println("Network traiined to error: " + e);
System.out.println("Saving network");
```

Regular Java Serialization code can be used to save the network or the **SerializeObject** class can be used. This utility class provides a **save** method that will write any single serializable object to a binary file. Here the **save** method is used to save the neural network.

```
   SerializeObject.save(FILENAME, network);
}
```

Now that the binary serialization file is created, load the neural network back from the file to see if it still performs well. This is performed by the **loadAndEvaluate** method.

```
public void loadAndEvaluate()
   throws IOException, ClassNotFoundException {
   System.out.println("Loading network");
```

The **SerializeObject** class also provides a **load** method that will read an object back from a binary serialization file.

```
BasicNetwork network =
   (BasicNetwork) SerializeObject.load(FILENAME);
MLDataSet trainingSet =
   new BasicMLDataSet(XOR_INPUT, XOR_IDEAL);
```

Now that the network is loaded, the error level is reported.

```
   double e = network.calculateError(trainingSet);
   System.out.println(
      "Loaded network's error is(should be same as above): " + e);
}
```

This error level should match the error level at the time the network was originally trained.

4.7   Summary

Feedforward and Simple Recurrent Neural Networks are created using the **BasicNetwork** and **BasicLayer** classes. Using these objects, neural networks can be created. Layers can also be connected using context links, just as simple recurrent neural networks, such as the Elman neural network, are created.

Encog uses activation functions to scale the output from neural network layers. By default, Encog will use a hyperbolic tangent function, which is a good general purposes activation function. Any class that acts as an activation function must implement the **ActivationFunction** interface. If the activation function is to be used with propagation training, the activation function must be able to calculate for its derivative.

The **ActivationBiPolar** activation function class is used when a network only accepts bipolar numbers. The **ActivationCompetitive** activation function class is used for competitive neural networks such as the self-organizing map. The **ActivationLinear** activation function class is used when no activation function is desired. The **ActivationLOG** activation function class works similarly to the **ActivationTANH** activation function class except it does not always saturate as a hidden layer. The **ActivationSigmoid** activation function class is similar to the **ActivationTANH** activation function class, except only positive numbers are returned. The **ActivationSoftMax** activation function class scales the output so that the sum is one.

This chapter illustrated how to persist Encog objects using two methods. Objects may be persisted by using either the Encog EG format or by Java serialization.

The Encog EG format is the preferred means for saving Encog neural networks. These objects are accessed using their resource name. The EG file can be interchanged between any platform that Encog supports.

Encog also allows Java serialization to store objects to disk or stream. Java serialization is more restrictive than Encog EG files. Because the binary files are automatically stored directly from the objects, even the smallest change to an Encog object can result in incompatible files. Additionally, other platforms will be unable to use the file.

In the next chapter the concept of neural network training is introduced. Training is the process where the weights of a neural network are modified to produce the desired output. There are several ways neural networks can be trained. The next chapter will introduce propagation training.

Chapter 5

Propagation Training

- How Propagation Training Works

- Propagation Training Types

- Training and Method Factories

- Multithreaded Training

Training is the means by which neural network weights are adjusted to give desirable outputs. This book will cover both supervised and unsupervised training. This chapter will discuss propagation training, a form of supervised training where the expected output is given to the training algorithm.

Encog also supports unsupervised training. With unsupervised training, the neural network is not provided with the expected output. Rather, the neural network learns and makes insights into the data with limited direction. Chapter 10 will discuss unsupervised training.

Propagation training can be a very effective form of training for feedforward, simple recurrent and other types of neural networks. While there are several different forms of propagation training, this chapter will focus on the forms of propagation currently supported by Encog. These six forms are listed as follows:

- Backpropagation Training

- Quick Propagation Training (QPROP)

- Manhattan Update Rule

- Resilient Propagation Training (RPROP)

- Scaled Conjugate Gradient (SCG)

- Levenberg Marquardt (LMA)

All six of these methods work somewhat similarly. However, there are some important differences. The next section will explore propagation training in general.

5.1   Understanding Propagation Training

Propagation training algorithms use supervised training. This means that the training algorithm is given a training set of inputs and the ideal output for each input. The propagation training algorithm will go through a series of iterations that will most likely improve the neural network's error rate by some degree. The error rate is the percent difference between the actual output from the neural network and the ideal output provided by the training data.

Each iteration will completely loop through the training data. For each item of training data, some change to the weight matrix will be calculated. These changes will be applied in batches using Encog's batch training. Therefore, Encog updates the weight matrix values at the end of an iteration.

Each training iteration begins by looping over all of the training elements in the training set. For each of these training elements, a two-pass process is executed: a forward pass and a backward pass.

The forward pass simply presents data to the neural network as it normally would if no training had occurred. The input data is presented and the algorithm calculates the error, i.e. the difference between the actual and ideal outputs. The output from each of the layers is also kept in this pass.

This allows the training algorithms to see the output from each of the neural network layers.

The backward pass starts at the output layer and works its way back to the input layer. The backward pass begins by examining the difference between each of the ideal and actual outputs from each of the neurons. The gradient of this error is then calculated. To calculate this gradient, the neural network's actual output is applied to the derivative of the activation function used for this level. This value is then multiplied by the error.

Because the algorithm uses the derivative function of the activation function, propagation training can only be used with activation functions that actually have a derivative function. This derivative calculates the error gradient for each connection in the neural network. How exactly this value is used depends on the training algorithm used.

5.1.1 Understanding Backpropagation

Backpropagation is one of the oldest training methods for feedforward neural networks. Backpropagation uses two parameters in conjunction with the gradient descent calculated in the previous section. The first parameter is the learning rate which is essentially a percent that determines how directly the gradient descent should be applied to the weight matrix. The gradient is multiplied by the learning rate and then added to the weight matrix. This slowly optimizes the weights to values that will produce a lower error.

One of the problems with the backpropagation algorithm is that the gradient descent algorithm will seek out local minima. These local minima are points of low error, but may not be a global minimum. The second parameter provided to the backpropagation algorithm helps the backpropagation out of local minima. The second parameter is called momentum. Momentum specifies to what degree the previous iteration weight changes should be applied to the current iteration.

The momentum parameter is essentially a percent, just like the learning rate. To use momentum, the backpropagation algorithm must keep track of what changes were applied to the weight matrix from the previous iteration. These changes will be reapplied to the current iteration, except scaled by the momentum parameters. Usually the momentum parameter will be less than one, so the weight changes from the previous training iteration are less significant than the changes calculated for the current iteration. For example, setting the momentum to 0.5 would cause 50% of the previous training iteration's changes to be applied to the weights for the current weight matrix.

The following code will setup a backpropagation trainer, given a training set and neural network.

```
Backpropagation train = new Backpropagation(network, trainingSet,
    0.7, 0.3);
```

The above code would create a backpropagation trainer with a learning rate of 0.7 and a momentum of 0.3. Once setup the training object is ready for iteration training. For an example of Encog iteration training see:

```
org.encog.examples.neural.xor.HelloWorld
```

The above example can easily be modified to use backpropagation training by replacing the resilient propagation training line with the above training line.

5.1.2   Understanding the Manhattan Update Rule

One of the problems with the backpropagation training algorithm is the degree to which the weights are changed. The gradient descent can often apply too large of a change to the weight matrix. The Manhattan Update Rule and resilient propagation training algorithms only use the sign of the gradient. The magnitude is discarded. This means it is only important if the gradient is positive, negative or near zero.

For the Manhattan Update Rule, this magnitude is used to determine how to update the weight matrix value. If the magnitude is near zero, then no change is made to the weight value. If the magnitude is positive, then the weight value is increased by a specific amount. If the magnitude is negative, then the weight value is decreased by a specific amount. The amount by which the weight value is changed is defined as a constant. You must provide this constant to the Manhattan Update Rule algorithm.

The following code will setup a Manhattan update trainer given a training set and neural network.

```
final ManhattanPropagation train =
  new ManhattanPropagation(network, trainingSet, 0.00001);
```

The above code would create a Manhattan Update Rule trainer with a learning rate of 0.00001. Manhattan propagation generally requires a small learning rate. Once setup is complete, the training object is ready for iteration training. For an example of Encog iteration training see:

```
org.encog.examples.neural.xor.HelloWorld
```

The above example can easily be modified to use Manhattan propagation training by replacing the resilient propagation training line with the above training line.

5.1.3 Understanding Quick Propagation Training

Quick propagation (QPROP) is another variant of propagation training. Quick propagation is based on Newton's Method, which is a means of finding a function's roots. This can be adapted to the task of minimizing the error of a neural network. Typically QPROP performs much better than backpropagation. The user must provide QPROP with a learning rate parameter. However, there is no momentum parameter as QPROP is typically more tolerant of higher learning rates. A learning rate of 2.0 is generally a good starting point.

The following code will setup a Quick Propagation trainer, given a training set and neural network.

```
QuickPropagation train =
  new QuickPropagation(network, trainingSet, 2.0);
```

The above code would create a QPROP trainer with a learning rate of 2.0. QPROP can generally take a higher learning rate. Once setup, the training object is ready for iteration training. For an example of Encog iteration training see:

```
org.encog.examples.neural.xor.HelloWorld
```

The above example can easily be modified to use QPROP training by replacing
the resilient propagation training line with the above training line.

5.1.4   Understanding Resilient Propagation Training

The resilient propagation training (RPROP) algorithm is often the most efficient training algorithm provided by Encog for supervised feedforward neural networks. One particular advantage to the RPROP algorithm is that it
requires no parameter setting before using it. There are no learning rates,
momentum values or update constants that need to be determined. This is
good because it can be difficult to determine the exact optimal learning rate.

The RPROP algorithms works similar to the Manhattan Update Rule in
that only the magnitude of the descent is used. However, rather than using a
fixed constant to update the weight values, a much more granular approach is
used. These deltas will not remain fixed like in the Manhattan Update Rule or
backpropagation algorithm. Rather, these delta values will change as training
progresses.

The RPROP algorithm does not keep one global update value, or delta.
Rather, individual deltas are kept for every weight matrix value. These deltas
are first initialized to a very small number. Every iteration through the
RPROP algorithm will update the weight values according to these delta values. However, as previously mentioned, these delta values do not remain fixed.
The gradient is used to determine how they should change using the magnitude to determine how the deltas should be modified further. This allows every
individual weight matrix value to be individually trained, an advantage not
provided by either the backpropagation algorithm or the Manhattan Update
Rule.

The following code will setup a Resilient Propagation trainer, given a training set and neural network.

```
ResilientPropagation train =
    new ResilientPropagation(network, trainingSet);
```

The above code would create a RPROP trainer. RPROP requires no parameters to be set to begin training. This is one of the main advantages of

the RPROP training algorithm. Once setup, the training object is ready for iteration training. For an example of Encog iteration training see:

```
org.encog.examples.neural.xor.HelloWorld
```

The above example already uses RPROP training.

There are four main variants of the RPROP algorithm that are supported by Encog:

- RPROP+

- RPROP-

- iRPROP+

- iPROP-

By default, Encog uses RPROP+, the most standard RPROP. Some research indicates that iRPROP+ is the most efficient RPROP algorithm. To set Encog to use iRPROP+ use the following command.

```
train.setRPROPType(RPROPType.iRPROPp);
```

5.1.5   Understanding SCG Training

Scaled Conjugate Gradient (SCG) is a fast and efficient training for Encog. SCG is based on a class of optimization algorithms called Conjugate Gradient Methods (CGM). SCG is not applicable for all data sets. When it is used within its applicability, it is quite efficient. Like RPROP, SCG is at an advantage as there are no parameters that must be set.

The following code will setup an SCG trainer, given a training set and neural network.

```
ScaledConjugateGradient train
  = new ScaledConjugateGradient(network, trainingSet);
```

The above code would create a SCG trainer. Once setup, the training object is ready for iteration training. For an example of Encog iteration training see:

```
org.encog.examples.neural.xor.HelloWorld
```

The above example can easily be modified to use SCG training by replacing the resilient propagation training line with the above training line.

5.1.6   Understanding LMA Training

The Levenberg Marquardt algorithm (LMA) is a very efficient training method for neural networks. In many cases, LMA will outperform Resilient Propagation. LMA is a hybrid algorithm based on both Newton's Method and gradient descent (backpropagation), integrating the strengths of both. Gradient descent is guaranteed to converge to a local minimum, albeit slowly. GNA is quite fast but often fails to converge. By using a damping factor to interpolate between the two, a hybrid method is created.

The following code shows how to use Levenberg-Marquardt with Encog for Java.

```
LevenbergMarquardtTraining  train = new LevenbergMarquardtTraining(
    network, trainingSet);
```

The above code would create an LMA with default parameters that likely require no adjustments. Once setup, the training object is ready for iteration training. For an example of Encog iteration training see:

```
org.encog.examples.neural.xor.HelloWorld
```

The above example can easily be modified to use LMA training by replacing the resilient propagation training line with the above training line.

5.2   Encog Method & Training Factories

This chapter illustrated how to instantiate trainers for many different training methods using objects such as **Backpropagation**, **ScaledConjugateGradient** or **ResilientPropagation**. In the previous chapters, we learned to create different types of neural networks using **BasicNetwork** and **BasicLayer**. We can also create training methods and neural networks using factories.

Factories create neural networks and training methods from text strings, saving time by eliminating the need to instantiate all of the objects otherwise necessary. For an example of factory usage see:

```
org.encog.examples.neural.xor.XORFactory
```

The above example uses factories to create both neural networks and training methods. This section will show how to create both neural networks and training methods using factories.

5.2.1   Creating Neural Networks with Factories

The following code uses a factory to create a feedforward neural network:

```
MLMethodFactory methodFactory = new MLMethodFactory();
MLMethod method = methodFactory.create(
    MLMethodFactory.TYPE_FEEDFORWARD,
    " ?:B->SIGMOID->4:B->SIGMOID->?" ,
    2,
    1);
```

The above code creates a neural network with two input neurons and one output neuron. There are four hidden neurons. Bias neurons are placed on the input and hidden layers. As is typical for neural networks, there are no bias neurons on the output layer. The sigmoid activation function is used between both the input and hidden neuron, as well between the hidden and output layer.

You may notice the two question marks in the neural network architecture string. These will be filled in by the input and output layer sizes specified in the create method and are optional. You can hard-code the input and output sizes. In this case the numbers specified in the create call will be ignored.

5.2.2   Creating Training Methods with Factories

It is also possible to create a training method using a factory. The following code creates a backpropagation trainer using a factory.

```
MLTrainFactory trainFactory = new MLTrainFactory();
MLTrain train = trainFactory.create(
  network,
  dataSet,
  MLTrainFactory.TYPE_BACKPROP,
  "LR=0.7,MOM=0.3"
  );
```

The above code creates a backpropagation trainer using a learning rate of 0.7 and a momentum of 0.3.

5.3   How Multithreaded Training Works

Multithreaded training works particularly well with larger training sets and machines multiple cores. If Encog does not detect that both are present, it will fall back to single-threaded. When there is more than one processing core and enough training set items to keep both busy, multithreaded training will function significantly faster than single-threaded.

This chapter has already introduced three propagation training techniques, all of which work similarly. Whether it is backpropagation, resilient propagation or the Manhattan Update Rule, the technique is similar. There are three distinct steps:

```
1. Perform a regular feed forward pass.
2. Process the levels backwards and determine the errors at each
   level.
3. Apply the changes to the weights.
```

First, a regular feed forward pass is performed. The output from each level is kept so the error for each level can be evaluated independently. Second, the errors are calculated at each level and the derivatives of each activation function are used to calculate gradient descents. These gradients show the direction that the weight must be modified to improve the error of the network. These gradients will be used in the third step.

The third step is what varies among the different training algorithms. Backpropagation simply scales the gradient descents by a learning rate. The scaled gradient descents are then directly applied to the weights. The Manhattan Update Rule only uses the gradient sign to decide in which direction to affect the weight. The weight is then changed in either the positive or negative direction by a fixed constant.

RPROP keeps an individual delta value for every weight and only uses the sign of the gradient descent to increase or decrease the delta amounts. The delta amounts are then applied to the weights.

The multithreaded algorithm uses threads to perform Steps 1 and 2. The training data is broken into packets that are distributed among the threads. At the beginning of each iteration, threads are started to handle each of these packets. Once all threads have completed, a single thread aggregates all of the results and applies them to the neural network. At the end of the iteration, there is a very brief amount of time where only one thread is executing. This can be seen from Figure 5.1.

Figure 5.1: Encog Training on a Hyperthreaded Quadcore

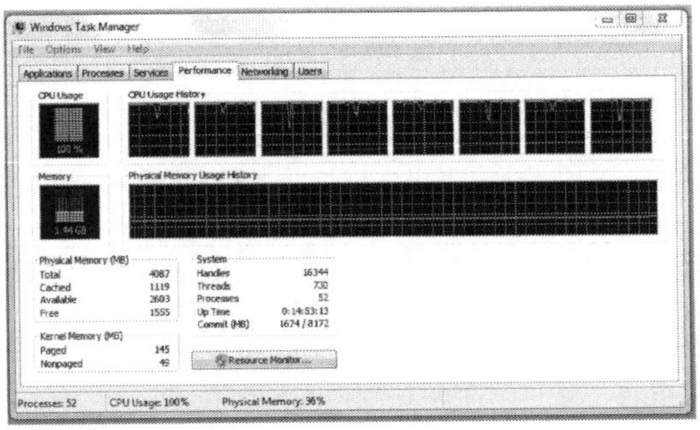

As shown in the above image, the i7 is currently running at 100%. The end of each iteration is clearly identified by where each of the processors falls briefly. Fortunately, this is a very brief time and does not have a large impact on overall training efficiency. In attempting to overcome this, various implementations tested not forcing the threads to wait at the end of the iteration for a resynchronization. This method did not provide efficient training because the propagation training algorithms need all changes applied before the next iteration begins.

5.4   Using Multithreaded Training

To see multithreaded training really shine, a larger training set is needed. In the next chapter we will see how to gather information for Encog using larger training sets. However, for now, we will look a simple benchmarking example that generates a random training set and compares multithreaded and single-threaded training times.

A simple benchmark is shown that makes use of an input layer of 40 neurons, a hidden layer of 60 neurons, and an output layer of 20 neurons. A training set of 50,000 elements is used. This example can be found at the following location.

```
org.encog.examples.neural.benchmark.MultiBench
```

Executing this program on a Quadcore i7 with Hyperthreading produced the following result:

```
Training 20 Iterations with Single-threaded
Iteration #1 Error:1.0594453784075148
Iteration #2 Error:1.0594453784075148
Iteration #3 Error:1.0059791059086385
Iteration #4 Error:0.955845375587124
Iteration #5 Error:0.934169803870454
Iteration #6 Error:0.9140418793336804
Iteration #7 Error:0.8950880473422747
Iteration #8 Error:0.8759150228219456
Iteration #9 Error:0.8596693523930371
Iteration #10 Error:0.843578483629412
Iteration #11 Error:0.8239688415389107
Iteration #12 Error:0.8076160458145523
Iteration #13 Error:0.7928442431442133
Iteration #14 Error:0.7772585699972144
Iteration #15 Error:0.7634533283610793
Iteration #16 Error:0.7500401666509937
Iteration #17 Error:0.7376158116045242
Iteration #18 Error:0.7268954113068246
Iteration #19 Error:0.7155784667628093
Iteration #20 Error:0.705537166118038
RPROP Result:35.134 seconds.
Final RPROP error: 0.6952141684716632
Training 20 Iterations with Multithreading
```

```
Iteration #1  Error:0.6952126315707992
Iteration #2  Error:0.6952126315707992
Iteration #3  Error:0.90915249248788
Iteration #4  Error:0.8797061675258835
Iteration #5  Error:0.8561169673033431
Iteration #6  Error:0.7909509694056177
Iteration #7  Error:0.7709539415065737
Iteration #8  Error:0.7541971172618358
Iteration #9  Error:0.7287094412886507
Iteration #10 Error:0.715814914438935
Iteration #11 Error:0.7037730808705016
Iteration #12 Error:0.6925902585055886
Iteration #13 Error:0.6784038181007823
Iteration #14 Error:0.6673310323078667
Iteration #15 Error:0.6585209150749294
Iteration #16 Error:0.6503710867148986
Iteration #17 Error:0.6429473784897797
Iteration #18 Error:0.6370962075614478
Iteration #19 Error:0.6314478792705961
Iteration #20 Error:0.6265724296587237
Multi-Threaded Result:8.793 seconds.
Final Multi-thread error: 0.6219704300851074
Factor improvement:4.0106783805299674
```

As shown by the above results, the single-threaded RPROP algorithm finished
in 128 seconds and the multithreaded RPROP algorithm finished in only 31
seconds. Multithreading improved performance by a factor of four. Your results running the above example will depend on how many cores your computer
has. If your computer is single core with no hyperthreading, then the factor
will be close to one. This is because the second multi-threading training will
fall back to a single thread.

5.5   Summary

This chapter explored how to use several propagation training algorithms with
Encog. Propagation training is a very common class of supervised training
algorithms. Resilient propagation training is usually the best choice; however,
the Manhattan Update Rule and backpropagation may be useful for certain
situations. SCG and QPROP are also solid training algorithms.

Backpropagation was one of the original training algorithms for feedforward neural networks. Though Encog supports it mostly for historic purposes, it can sometimes be used to further refine a neural network after resilient propagation has been used. Backpropagation uses a learning rate and momentum. The learning rate defines how quickly the neural network will learn; the momentum helps the network get out of local minima.

The Manhattan Update Rule uses a delta value to update the weight values. It can be difficult to choose this delta value correctly; too high of a value will cause the network to learn nothing at all.

Resilient propagation (RPROP) is one of the best training algorithms offered by Encog. It does not require you to provide training parameters, like the other two propagation training algorithms. This makes it much easier to use. Additionally, resilient propagation is considerably more efficient than Manhattan Update Rule or backpropagation.

SCG and QPROP are also very effective training methods. SCG does not work well for all sets training data, but it is very effective when it does work. QPROP works similar to RPROP. It can be an effective training method. However, QPROP requires the user to choose a learning rate.

Multithreaded training is a training technique that adapts propagation training to perform faster with multicore computers. Given a computer with multiple cores and a large enough training set, multithreaded training is considerably faster than single-threaded training. Encog can automatically set an optimal number of threads. If these conditions are not present, Encog will fall back to single-threaded training.

Propagation training is not the only type of supervised training that can be used with Encog. The next chapter introduces some other types of training algorithms used for supervised training. It will also explore how to use training techniques such as simulated annealing and genetic algorithms.

Chapter 6

More Supervised Training

- Introducing the Lunar Lander Example

- Supervised Training without Training Sets

- Using Genetic Algorithms

- Using Simulated Annealing

- Genetic Algorithms and Simulated Annealing with Training Sets

So far, this book has only explored training a neural network by using the supervised propagation training methods. This chapter will look at some non-propagation training techniques. The neural network in this chapter will be trained without a training set. It is still supervised in that feedback from the neural network's output is constantly used to help train the neural network. We simply will not supply training data ahead of time.

Two common techniques for this sort of training are simulated annealing and genetic algorithms. Encog provides built-in support for both. The example in this chapter can be trained with either algorithm, both of which will be discussed later in this chapter.

The example in this chapter presents the classic "Lunar Lander" game. This game has been implemented many times and is almost as old as computers themselves. You can read more about the Lunar Lander game on Wikipedia.

http://en.wikipedia.org/wiki/Lunar_Lander_%28computer_game%29

The idea behind most variants of the Lunar Lander game is very similar and the example program works as follows: The lunar lander spacecraft will begin to fall. As it falls, it accelerates. There is a maximum velocity that the lander can reach, which is called the 'terminal velocity.' Thrusters can be applied to the lander to slow its descent. However, there is a limited amount of fuel. Once the fuel is exhausted, the lander will simply fall, and nothing can be done.

This chapter will teach a neural network to pilot the lander. This is a very simple text-only simulation. The neural network will have only one option available to it. It can either decide to fire the thrusters or not to fire the thrusters. No training data will be created ahead of time and no assumptions will be made about how the neural network should pilot the craft. If using training sets, input would be provided ahead of time regarding what the neural network should do in certain situations. For this example, the neural network will learn everything on its own.

Even though the neural network will learn everything on its own, this is still supervised training. The neural network will not be totally left to its own devices. It will receive a way to score the neural network. To score the neural network, we must give it some goals and then calculate a numeric value that determines how well the neural network achieved its goals.

These goals are arbitrary and simply reflect what was picked to score the network. The goals are summarized here:

- Land as softly as possible

- Cover as much distance as possible

- Conserve fuel

The first goal is not to crash, but to try to hit the lunar surface as softly as possible. Therefore, any velocity at the time of impact is a very big negative score. The second goal for the neural network is to try to cover as much distance as possible while falling. To do this, it needs to stay aloft as long as possible and additional points are awarded for staying aloft longer. Finally, bonus points are given for still having fuel once the craft lands. The score calculation can be seen in Equation 6.1.

$$\text{score} = (\text{fuel} \cdot 10) + (\text{velocity} \cdot 1000) + \text{fuel} \qquad (6.1)$$

In the next section we will run the Lunar Lander example and observe as it learns to land a spacecraft.

6.1   Running the Lunar Lander Example

To run the Lunar Lander game you should execute the **LunarLander** class. This class is located at the following location.

```
org.encog.examples.neural.lunar.LunarLander
```

This class requires no arguments. Once the program begins, the neural network immediately begins training. It will cycle through 50 epochs, or training iterations, before it is done. When it first begins, the score is a negative number. These early attempts by the untrained neural network are hitting the moon at high velocity and are not covering much distance.

```
Epoch #1 Score:-299.0
Epoch #2 Score:-299.0
Epoch #3 Score:-299.0
Epoch #4 Score:-299.0
Epoch #5 Score:-299.0
Epoch #6 Score:-299.0
Epoch #7 Score:-299.0
```

After the seventh epoch, the score begins to increase.

```
Epoch #8 Score:-96.0
Epoch #9 Score:5760.0
Epoch #10 Score:5760.0
Epoch #11 Score:5760.0
Epoch #12 Score:5760.0
Epoch #13 Score:5760.0
Epoch #14 Score:5760.0
Epoch #15 Score:5760.0
```

```
Epoch #16  Score:5760.0
Epoch #17  Score:6196.0
Epoch #18  Score:6196.0
Epoch #19  Score:6196.0
```

The score will hover at 6,196 for awhile, but will improve at a later epoch.

```
Epoch #45  Score:6275.0
Epoch #46  Score:6275.0
Epoch #47  Score:7347.0
Epoch #48  Score:7347.0
Epoch #49  Score:7460.0
Epoch #50  Score:7460.0
```

By the 50th epoch, a score of 7,460 has been achieved. The training techniques used in this chapter make extensive use of random numbers. As a result, running this example multiple times may result in entirely different scores.

More epochs may have produced a better-trained neural network; however, the program limits it to 50. This number usually produces a fairly skilled neural pilot. Once the network is trained, run the simulation with the winning pilot. The telemetry is displayed at each second.

The neural pilot kept the craft aloft for 911 seconds. So, we will not show every telemetry report. However, some of the interesting actions that this neural pilot learned are highlighted. The neural network learned it was best to just let the craft free-fall for awhile.

```
How the winning network landed:
Elapsed:  1 s, Fuel: 200 l, Velocity:  -1.6200 m/s, 9998 m
Elapsed:  2 s, Fuel: 200 l, Velocity:  -3.2400 m/s, 9995 m
Elapsed:  3 s, Fuel: 200 l, Velocity:  -4.8600 m/s, 9990 m
Elapsed:  4 s, Fuel: 200 l, Velocity:  -6.4800 m/s, 9983 m
Elapsed:  5 s, Fuel: 200 l, Velocity:  -8.1000 m/s, 9975 m
Elapsed:  6 s, Fuel: 200 l, Velocity:  -9.7200 m/s, 9965 m
Elapsed:  7 s, Fuel: 200 l, Velocity: -11.3400 m/s, 9954 m
Elapsed:  8 s, Fuel: 200 l, Velocity: -12.9600 m/s, 9941 m
Elapsed:  9 s, Fuel: 200 l, Velocity: -14.5800 m/s, 9927 m
Elapsed: 10 s, Fuel: 200 l, Velocity: -16.2000 m/s, 9910 m
Elapsed: 11 s, Fuel: 200 l, Velocity: -17.8200 m/s, 9893 m
Elapsed: 12 s, Fuel: 200 l, Velocity: -19.4400 m/s, 9873 m
Elapsed: 13 s, Fuel: 200 l, Velocity: -21.0600 m/s, 9852 m
Elapsed: 14 s, Fuel: 200 l, Velocity: -22.6800 m/s, 9829 m
```

```
Elapsed:  15 s, Fuel: 200 l, Velocity: −24.3000 m/s, 9805 m
Elapsed:  16 s, Fuel: 200 l, Velocity: −25.9200 m/s, 9779 m
Elapsed:  17 s, Fuel: 200 l, Velocity: −27.5400 m/s, 9752 m
Elapsed:  18 s, Fuel: 200 l, Velocity: −29.1600 m/s, 9722 m
Elapsed:  19 s, Fuel: 200 l, Velocity: −30.7800 m/s, 9692 m
Elapsed:  20 s, Fuel: 200 l, Velocity: −32.4000 m/s, 9659 m
Elapsed:  21 s, Fuel: 200 l, Velocity: −34.0200 m/s, 9625 m
Elapsed:  22 s, Fuel: 200 l, Velocity: −35.6400 m/s, 9590 m
Elapsed:  23 s, Fuel: 200 l, Velocity: −37.2600 m/s, 9552 m
Elapsed:  24 s, Fuel: 200 l, Velocity: −38.8800 m/s, 9514 m
Elapsed:  25 s, Fuel: 200 l, Velocity: −40.0000 m/s, 9473 m
Elapsed:  26 s, Fuel: 200 l, Velocity: −40.0000 m/s, 9431 m
Elapsed:  27 s, Fuel: 200 l, Velocity: −40.0000 m/s, 9390 m
```

You can see that 27 seconds in and 9,390 meters above the ground, the terminal velocity of -40 m/s has been reached. There is no real science behind -40 m/s being the terminal velocity; it was just chosen as an arbitrary number. Having a terminal velocity is interesting because the neural networks learn that once this is reached, the craft will not speed up. They use the terminal velocity to save fuel and "break their fall" when they get close to the surface. The freefall at terminal velocity continues for some time.

Finally, at 6,102 meters above the ground, the thrusters are fired for the first time.

```
Elapsed: 105 s, Fuel: 200 l, Velocity: −40.0000 m/s, 6143 m
Elapsed: 106 s, Fuel: 200 l, Velocity: −40.0000 m/s, 6102 m
THRUST
Elapsed: 107 s, Fuel: 199 l, Velocity: −31.6200 m/s, 6060 m
Elapsed: 108 s, Fuel: 199 l, Velocity: −33.2400 m/s, 6027 m
Elapsed: 109 s, Fuel: 199 l, Velocity: −34.8600 m/s, 5992 m
Elapsed: 110 s, Fuel: 199 l, Velocity: −36.4800 m/s, 5956 m
Elapsed: 111 s, Fuel: 199 l, Velocity: −38.1000 m/s, 5917 m
Elapsed: 112 s, Fuel: 199 l, Velocity: −39.7200 m/s, 5878 m
THRUST
Elapsed: 113 s, Fuel: 198 l, Velocity: −31.3400 m/s, 5836 m
Elapsed: 114 s, Fuel: 198 l, Velocity: −32.9600 m/s, 5803 m
Elapsed: 115 s, Fuel: 198 l, Velocity: −34.5800 m/s, 5769 m
Elapsed: 116 s, Fuel: 198 l, Velocity: −36.2000 m/s, 5733 m
Elapsed: 117 s, Fuel: 198 l, Velocity: −37.8200 m/s, 5695 m
```

The velocity is gradually slowed, as the neural network decides to fire the thrusters every six seconds. This keeps the velocity around -35 m/s.

```
THRUST
Elapsed:  118 s,  Fuel:  197 l,  Velocity:  −29.4400 m/s,  5655 m
Elapsed:  119 s,  Fuel:  197 l,  Velocity:  −31.0600 m/s,  5624 m
Elapsed:  120 s,  Fuel:  197 l,  Velocity:  −32.6800 m/s,  5592 m
Elapsed:  121 s,  Fuel:  197 l,  Velocity:  −34.3000 m/s,  5557 m
Elapsed:  122 s,  Fuel:  197 l,  Velocity:  −35.9200 m/s,  5521 m
THRUST
Elapsed:  123 s,  Fuel:  196 l,  Velocity:  −27.5400 m/s,  5484 m
Elapsed:  124 s,  Fuel:  196 l,  Velocity:  −29.1600 m/s,  5455 m
Elapsed:  125 s,  Fuel:  196 l,  Velocity:  −30.7800 m/s,  5424 m
Elapsed:  126 s,  Fuel:  196 l,  Velocity:  −32.4000 m/s,  5392 m
Elapsed:  127 s,  Fuel:  196 l,  Velocity:  −34.0200 m/s,  5358 m
Elapsed:  128 s,  Fuel:  196 l,  Velocity:  −35.6400 m/s,  5322 m
THRUST
```

As the craft gets closer to the lunar surface, this maximum allowed velocity begins to decrease. The pilot is slowing the craft, as it gets closer to the lunar surface. At around 4,274 meters above the surface, the neural network decides it should now thrust every five seconds. This slows the descent to around -28 m/s.

```
THRUST
Elapsed:  163 s,  Fuel:  189 l,  Velocity:  −22.3400 m/s,  4274 m
Elapsed:  164 s,  Fuel:  189 l,  Velocity:  −23.9600 m/s,  4250 m
Elapsed:  165 s,  Fuel:  189 l,  Velocity:  −25.5800 m/s,  4224 m
Elapsed:  166 s,  Fuel:  189 l,  Velocity:  −27.2000 m/s,  4197 m
Elapsed:  167 s,  Fuel:  189 l,  Velocity:  −28.8200 m/s,  4168 m
THRUST
Elapsed:  168 s,  Fuel:  188 l,  Velocity:  −20.4400 m/s,  4138 m
Elapsed:  169 s,  Fuel:  188 l,  Velocity:  −22.0600 m/s,  4116 m
Elapsed:  170 s,  Fuel:  188 l,  Velocity:  −23.6800 m/s,  4092 m
Elapsed:  171 s,  Fuel:  188 l,  Velocity:  −25.3000 m/s,  4067 m
Elapsed:  172 s,  Fuel:  188 l,  Velocity:  −26.9200 m/s,  4040 m
Elapsed:  173 s,  Fuel:  188 l,  Velocity:  −28.5400 m/s,  4011 m
THRUST
```

By occasionally using shorter cycles, the neural pilot slows it even further by the time it reaches only 906 meters above the surface. The craft has been slowed to -14 meters per second.

```
THRUST
Elapsed: 320 s, Fuel: 162 l, Velocity: -6.6800 m/s, 964 m
Elapsed: 321 s, Fuel: 162 l, Velocity: -8.3000 m/s, 955 m
Elapsed: 322 s, Fuel: 162 l, Velocity: -9.9200 m/s, 945 m
Elapsed: 323 s, Fuel: 162 l, Velocity: -11.5400 m/s, 934 m
Elapsed: 324 s, Fuel: 162 l, Velocity: -13.1600 m/s, 921 m
Elapsed: 325 s, Fuel: 162 l, Velocity: -14.7800 m/s, 906 m
THRUST
Elapsed: 326 s, Fuel: 161 l, Velocity: -6.4000 m/s, 890 m
Elapsed: 327 s, Fuel: 161 l, Velocity: -8.0200 m/s, 882 m
Elapsed: 328 s, Fuel: 161 l, Velocity: -9.6400 m/s, 872 m
Elapsed: 329 s, Fuel: 161 l, Velocity: -11.2600 m/s, 861 m
Elapsed: 330 s, Fuel: 161 l, Velocity: -12.8800 m/s, 848 m
Elapsed: 331 s, Fuel: 161 l, Velocity: -14.5000 m/s, 833 m
THRUST
```

This short cycling continues until the craft has slowed its velocity considerably. It even thrusts to the point of increasing its altitude towards the final seconds of the flight.

```
Elapsed: 899 s, Fuel: 67 l, Velocity: 5.3400 m/s, 2 m
Elapsed: 900 s, Fuel: 67 l, Velocity: 3.7200 m/s, 5 m
Elapsed: 901 s, Fuel: 67 l, Velocity: 2.1000 m/s, 8 m
Elapsed: 902 s, Fuel: 67 l, Velocity: 0.4800 m/s, 8 m
Elapsed: 903 s, Fuel: 67 l, Velocity: -1.1400 m/s, 7 m
Elapsed: 904 s, Fuel: 67 l, Velocity: -2.7600 m/s, 4 m
THRUST
Elapsed: 905 s, Fuel: 66 l, Velocity: 5.6200 m/s, 0 m
Elapsed: 906 s, Fuel: 66 l, Velocity: 4.0000 m/s, 4 m
Elapsed: 907 s, Fuel: 66 l, Velocity: 2.3800 m/s, 6 m
Elapsed: 908 s, Fuel: 66 l, Velocity: 0.7600 m/s, 7 m
Elapsed: 909 s, Fuel: 66 l, Velocity: -0.8600 m/s, 6 m
Elapsed: 910 s, Fuel: 66 l, Velocity: -2.4800 m/s, 4 m
THRUST
Elapsed: 911 s, Fuel: 65 l, Velocity: 5.9000 m/s, 0 m
```

Finally, the craft lands, with a very soft velocity of positive 5.9.

You wonder why the lander lands with a velocity of 5.9. This is due to a slight glitch in the program. This "glitch" is left in because it illustrates an important point: when neural networks are allowed to learn, they are totally on their own and will take advantage of everything they can find.

The final positive velocity is because the program decides if it wants to thrust as the last part of a simulation cycle. The program has already decided the craft's altitude is below zero, and it has landed. But the neural network "sneaks in" that one final thrust, even though the craft is already landed and this thrust does no good. However, the final thrust does increase the score of the neural network.

Recall equation 6.1. For every negative meter per second of velocity at landing, the program score is decreased by 1,000. The program figured out that the opposite is also true. For every positive meter per second of velocity, it also gains 1,000 points. By learning about this little quirk in the program, the neural pilot can obtain even higher scores.

The neural pilot learned some very interesting things without being fed a pre-devised strategy. The network learned what it wanted to do. Specifically, this pilot decided the following:

- Free-fall for some time to take advantage of terminal velocity.

- At a certain point, break the freefall and slow the craft.

- Slowly lose speed as you approach the surface.

- Give one final thrust, after landing, to maximize score.

The neural pilot in this example was trained using a genetic algorithm. Genetic algorithms and simulated annealing will be discussed later in this chapter. First, we will see how the Lander was simulated and how its score is actually calculated.

6.2   Examining the Lunar Lander Simulator

We will now examine how the Lunar Lander example was created by physical simulation and how the neural network actually pilots the spacecraft. Finally, we will see how the neural network learns to be a better pilot.

6.2.1 Simulating the Lander

First, we need a class that will simulate the "physics" of lunar landing. The term "physics" is used very loosely. The purpose of this example is more on how a neural network adapts to an artificial environment than any sort of realistic physical simulation.

All of the physical simulation code is contained in the **LanderSimulator** class. This class can be found at the following location.

```
org.encog.examples.neural.lunar.LanderSimulator
```

This class begins by defining some constants that will be important to the simulation.

```
public static final double GRAVITY = 1.62;
public static final double THRUST = 10;
public static final double TERMINAL_VELOCITY = 40;
```

The **GRAVITY** constant defines the acceleration on the moon that is due to gravity. It is set to 1.62 and is measured in meters per second. The **THRUST** constant specifies how the number of meters per second by which the gravity acceleration will be countered. The **TERMINAL_VELOCITY** is the fastest speed that the spacecraft can travel either upward or downward.

In addition to these constants, the simulator program will need several instance variables to maintain state. These variables are listed below as follows:

```
private int fuel;
private int seconds;
private double altitude;
private double velocity;
```

The **fuel** variable holds the amount of fuel remaining. The **seconds** variable holds the number of seconds aloft. The **altitude** variable holds the current altitude in meters. The **velocity** variable holds the current velocity. Positive numbers indicate that the craft is moving upwards. Negative numbers indicate that the craft is moving downwards.

The simulator sets the values to reasonable starting values in the following constructor:

```
public LanderSimulator() {
  this.fuel = 200;
  this.seconds = 0;
  this.altitude = 10000;
  this.velocity = 0;
}
```

The craft starts with 200 liters and the altitude is set to 10,000 meters above ground.

The **turn** method processes each "turn." A turn is one second in the simulator. The **thrust** parameter indicates whether the spacecraft wishes to thrust during this turn.

```
public void turn(boolean thrust) {
```

First, increase the number of seconds elapsed by one. Decrease the velocity by the **GRAVITY** constant to simulate the fall.

```
  this.seconds++;
  this.velocity -=GRAVITY;
```

The current velocity increases the altitude. Of course, if the velocity is negative, the altitude will decrease.

```
  this.altitude+=this.velocity;
```

If thrust is applied during this turn, then decrease the **fuel** by one and increase the velocity by the **THRUST** constant.

```
  if( thrust && this.fuel >0 ) {
    this.fuel --;
    this.velocity+=THRUST;
  }
```

Terminal velocity must be imposed as it cannot fall or ascend faster than the terminal velocity. The following line makes sure that the lander is not ascending faster than the terminal velocity.

```
  this.velocity = Math.max(
    -TERMINAL_VELOCITY,
    this.velocity );
```

The following line makes sure that we are not descending faster than the terminal velocity.

```
this.velocity = Math.min(
   TERMINAL_VELOCITY,
   this.velocity);
```

The following line makes sure that the altitude does not drop below zero. It is important to prevent the simulation of the craft hitting so hard that it goes underground.

```
if( this.altitude <0)
   this.altitude = 0;
}
```

In addition to the simulation code, the **LanderSimulator** also provides two utility functions. The first calculates the score and should only be called after the spacecraft lands. This method is shown here.

```
public int score() {
   return (int)((this.fuel*10)
     + this.seconds
     + (this.velocity*1000));
}
```

The **score** method implements Equation 6.1. As you can see, it uses **fuel**, **seconds** and **velocity** to calculate the score according to the earlier equation.

Additionally, a method is provided to determine if the spacecraft is still flying. If the altitude is greater than zero, it is still flying.

```
public boolean flying() {
   return(this.altitude >0);
}
```

In the next section, we will see how the neural network actually flies the spacecraft and is given a score.

6.2.2   Calculating the Score

The **PilotScore** class implements the code necessary for the neural network
to fly the spacecraft. This class also calculates the final score after the craft
has landed. This class is shown in Listing 6.1.

Listing 6.1: Calculating the Lander Score

```java
package org.encog.examples.neural.lunar;
import org.encog.neural.networks.BasicNetwork;
import org.encog.neural.networks.training.CalculateScore;
public class PilotScore implements CalculateScore {
  public double calculateScore(BasicNetwork network) {
    NeuralPilot pilot = new NeuralPilot(network, false);
    return pilot.scorePilot();
  }
  public boolean shouldMinimize() {
    return false;
  }
}
```

As you can see from the following line, the **PilotScore** class implements the
CalculateScore interface.

```java
public class PilotScore implements CalculateScore {
```

The **CalculateScore** interface is used by both Encog simulated annealing and
genetic algorithms to determine how effective a neural network is at solving
the given problem. A low score could be either bad or good depending on the
problem.

   The **CalculateScore** interface requires two methods. This first method is
named **calculateNetworkScore**. This method accepts a neural network and
returns a **double** that represents the score of the network.

```java
public double calculateNetworkScore(
  BasicNetwork network) {
  NeuralPilot pilot = new NeuralPilot(network, false);
  return pilot.scorePilot();
}
```

The second method returns a value to indicate if the score should be minimized.

```
public boolean shouldMinimize() {
    return false;
}
```

For this example we would like to maximize the score. As a result the **should-Minimize** method returns **false**.

6.2.3   Flying the Spacecraft

This section shows how the neural network actually flies the spacecraft. The neural network will be fed environmental information such as fuel remaining, altitude and current velocity. The neural network will then output a single value that will indicate if the neural network wishes to thrust. The **NeuralPilot** class performs this flight. You can see the **NeuralPilot** class at the following location:

```
org.encog.examples.neural.lunar.NeuralPilot
```

The **NeuralPilot** constructor sets up the pilot to fly the spacecraft. The constructor is passed a network to fly the spacecraft, as well as a Boolean that indicates if telemetry should be tracked to the screen.

```
public NeuralPilot(
    BasicNetwork network, boolean track) {
```

The lunar lander must feed the fuel level, altitude and current velocity to the neural network. These values must be normalized as was covered in Chapter 2. To perform this normalization, the constructor begins by setting several normalization fields.

```
private NormalizedField fuelStats;
private NormalizedField altitudeStats;
private NormalizedField velocityStats;
```

In addition to the normalized fields, we will also save the operating parameters. The **track** variable is saved to the instance level so that the program will later know if it should display telemetry.

```
this.track = track;
this.network = network;
```

The neural pilot will have three input neurons and one output neuron. These three input neurons will communicate the following three fields to the neural network.

- Current fuel level

- Current altitude

- Current velocity

These three input fields will produce one output field that indicates if the neural pilot would like to fire the thrusters.

To normalize these three fields, define them as three **NormalizedField** objects. First, set up the fuel.

```
fuelStats =
  new NormalizedField(
    NormalizationAction.Normalize,
    "fuel",
    200,
    0,
    -0.9,
    0.9);
```

We know that the range is between 0 and 200 for the fuel. We will normalize this to the range of -0.9 to 10.9. This is very similar to the range -1 to 1, except it does not take the values all the way to the extreme. This will sometimes help the neural network to learn better. Especially when the full range is known.

Next velocity and altitude are set up.

```
altitudeStats =
  new NormalizedField(
    NormalizationAction.Normalize,
    "altitude",
    10000,
    0,
    -0.9,
    0.9);
```

Velocity and altitude both have known ranges just like fuel. As a result, velocity is set up similarly to fuel and altitude.

```
velocityStats =
  new NormalizedField(NormalizationAction.Normalize,
    "velocity",
    LanderSimulator.TERMINAL_VELOCITY,
    -LanderSimulator.TERMINAL_VELOCITY, -0.9, 0.9);
```

Because we do not have training data, it is very important that we know the ranges. This is unlike the examples in Chapter 2 that provided sample data to determine minimum and maximum values.

For this example, the primary purpose of flying the spacecraft is to receive a score. The **scorePilot** method calculates this score. It will simulate a flight from the point that the spacecraft is dropped from the orbiter to the point that it lands. The **scorePilot** method calculates this score:

```
public int scorePilot() {
```

This method begins by creating a **LanderSimulator** object to simulate the very simple physics used by this program.

```
LanderSimulator sim = new LanderSimulator();
```

We now enter the main loop of the **scorePilot** method. It will continue looping as long as the spacecraft is still flying. The spacecraft is still flying as long as its altitude is greater than zero.

```
while(sim.flying()) {
```

Begin by creating an array to hold the raw data that is obtained directly from the simulator.

```
MLData input = new BasicMLData(3);
input.setData(0, this.fuelStats.normalize(sim.getFuel()));
input.setData(1, this.altitudeStats.normalize(sim.getAltitude()));
input.setData(2, this.velocityStats.normalize(sim.getVelocity()));
```

The **normalize** method of the **NormalizedField** object is used to actually normalize the files of fuel, altitude and velocity.

```
MLData output = this.network.compute(input);
```

This single output neuron will determine if the thrusters should be fired.

```
double value = output.getData(0);
boolean thrust;
```

If the value is greater than zero, then the thrusters will be fired. If the spacecraft is tracking, then also display that the thrusters were fired.

```
if( value > 0 ) {
   thrust = true;
   if( track )
      System.out.println("THRUST");
}
else
   thrust = false;
```

Process the next "turn" in the simulator and thrust if necessary. Also display telemetry if the spacecraft is tracking.

```
sim.turn(thrust);
if( track )
   System.out.println(sim.telemetry());
}
```

The spacecraft has now landed. Return the score based on the criteria previously discussed.

```
return(sim.cost());
```

We will now look at how to train the neural pilot.

6.3 Training the Neural Pilot

This example can train the neural pilot using either a genetic algorithm or simulated annealing. Encog treats both genetic algorithms and simulated annealing very similarly. On one hand, you can simply provide a training set and use simulated annealing or you can use a genetic algorithm just as in a propagation network. We will see an example of this later in the chapter as we apply these two techniques to the XOR problem. This will show how similar they can be to propagation training.

On the other hand, genetic algorithms and simulated annealing can do something that propagation training cannot. They can allow you to train without a training set. It is still supervised training since a scoring class is used, as developed earlier in this chapter. However, it still does not need to training data input. Rather, the neural network needs input on how good of a job it is doing. If you can provide this scoring function, simulated annealing or a genetic algorithm can train the neural network. Both methods will be discussed in the coming sections, beginning with a genetic algorithm.

6.3.1 What is a Genetic Algorithm

Genetic algorithms attempt to simulate Darwinian evolution to create a better neural network. The neural network is reduced to an array of **double** variables. This array becomes the genetic sequence.

The genetic algorithm begins by creating a population of random neural networks. All neural networks in this population have the same structure, meaning they have the same number of neurons and layers. However, they all have different random weights.

These neural networks are sorted according their "scores." Their scores are provided by the scoring method as discussed in the last section. In the case of the neural pilot, this score indicates how softly the ship landed.

The top neural networks are selected to "breed." The bottom neural networks "die." When two networks breed, nature is simulated by splicing their DNA. In this case, splices are taken from the double array from each network and spliced together to create a new offspring neural network. The offspring neural networks take up the places vacated by the dying neural networks.

Some of the offspring will be "mutated." That is, some of the genetic material will be random and not from either parent. This introduces needed variety into the gene pool and simulates the natural process of mutation.

The population is sorted and the process begins again. Each iteration provides one cycle. As you can see, there is no need for a training set. All that is needed is an object to score each neural network. Of course you can use training sets by simply providing a scoring object that uses a training set to score each network.

6.3.2   Using a Genetic Algorithm

Using the genetic algorithm is very easy and uses the **NeuralGeneticAlgorithm** class to do this. The **NeuralGeneticAlgorithm** class implements the **MLTrain** interface. Therefore, once constructed, it is used in the same way as any other Encog training class.

The following code creates a new **NeuralGeneticAlgorithm** to train the neural pilot.

```
train = new NeuralGeneticAlgorithm(
  network, new NguyenWidrowRandomizer (),
  new PilotScore(),500, 0.1, 0.25);
```

The base network is provided to communicate the structure of the neural network to the genetic algorithm. The genetic algorithm will disregard weights currently set by the neural network.

The randomizer is provided so that the neural network can create a new random population. The **NguyenWidrowRandomizer** attempts to produce starting weights that are less extreme and more trainable than the regular **RangeRandomizer** that is usually used. However, either randomizer could be used.

The value of 500 specifies the population size. Larger populations will train better, but will take more memory and processing time. The 0.1 is used to mutate 10% of the offspring. The 0.25 value is used to choose the mating population from the top 25% of the population.

```
int epoch = 1;
```

Now that the trainer is set up, the neural network is trained just like any Encog training object. Here we only iterate 50 times. This is usually enough to produce a skilled neural pilot.

```
for(int i=0;i<50;i++) {
  train.iteration();
  System.out.println(
  "Epoch #" + epoch + " Score:" + train.getError());
  epoch++;
}
```

This neural network could have also trained using the **EncogUtility** class, as in the previous chapter. Just for simple training, the **EncogUtility** is usually the preferred method. However, if your program needs to do something after each iteration, the more manual approach shown above may be preferable.

6.3.3 What is Simulated Annealing

Simulated annealing can also be used to train the neural pilot. Simulated annealing is similar to a genetic algorithm in that it needs a scoring object. However, it works quite differently internally. Simulated annealing simulates the metallurgical process of annealing.

Annealing is the process by which a very hot molten metal is slowly cooled. This slow cooling process causes the metal to produce a strong, consistent molecular structure. Annealing is a process that produces metals less likely to fracture or shatter.

A similar process can be performed on neural networks. To implement simulated annealing, the neural network is converted to an array of double values. This is exactly the same process as was done for the genetic algorithm.

Randomness is used to simulate the heat and cooling effect. While the neural network is still really "hot," the neural network's existing weights increase in speed. As the network cools, this randomness slows down. Only changes that produce a positive effect on the network's score are kept.

6.3.4 Using Simulated Annealing

To use simulated annealing to train the neural pilot, pass the argument anneal on the command line when running this example. It is very simple for the example to use annealing rather than a genetic algorithm. They both use the same scoring function and are interchangeable. The following lines of code make use of the simulated annealing algorithm for this example.

```
if ( args.length >0 && args [0].equalsIgnoreCase("anneal"))
{
   train = new NeuralSimulatedAnnealing(
network, new PilotScore(), 10, 2, 100);
```

```
}
```

The simulated annealing object **NeuralSimulatedAnnealing** is used to train the neural pilot. The neural network is passed along with the same scoring object that was used to train using a genetic algorithm.

The values of 10 and 2 are the starting and stopping temperatures, respectively. They are not true temperatures, in terms of Fahrenheit or Celsius. A higher number will produce more randomness; a lower number produces less randomness. The following code shows how this temperature or factor is applied.

```
public final void randomize() {
  final double[] array = NetworkCODEC
  .networkToArray(NeuralSimulatedAnnealing.this.network);
  for (int i = 0; i < array.length; i++) {
    double add = NeuralSimulatedAnnealing.CUT − Math.random();
    add /= this.anneal.getStartTemperature();
    add *= this.anneal.getTemperature();
    array[i] = array[i] + add;
  }
NetworkCODEC.arrayToNetwork(array,
  NeuralSimulatedAnnealing.this.network);
}
```

The number 100 specifies how many cycles, per iteration, that it should take to go from the higher temperature to the lower temperature. Generally, the more cycles, the more accurate the results will be. However, the higher the number, the longer it takes to train.

There are no simple rules for how to set these values. Generally, it is best to experiment with different values to see which trains your particular neural network the best.

6.4 Using the Training Set Score Class

Training sets can also be used with genetic algorithms and simulated annealing. Used this way, simulated annealing and genetic algorithms are a little different than propagation training based on usage. There is no scoring function when used this way. You simply use the **TrainingSetScore** object, which takes the training set and uses it to score the neural network.

Generally resilient propagation will outperform genetic algorithms or simulated annealing when used in this way. Genetic algorithms or simulated annealing really excel when using a scoring method instead of a training set. Furthermore, simulated annealing can sometimes to push backpropagation out of a local minimum.

The Hello World application, found at the following location, could easily be modified to use a genetic algorithm or simulated annealing:

```
org.encog.examples.neural.xor.HelloWorld
```

To change the above example to use a genetic algorithm, a few lines must be added. The following lines create a training set-based genetic algorithm. First, create a **TrainingSetScore** object.

```
CalculateScore score = new TrainingSetScore(trainingSet);
```

This object can then be used with either a genetic algorithm or simulated annealing. The following code shows it being used with a genetic algorithm:

```
final MLTrain train = new NeuralGeneticAlgorithm(
   network, new NguyenWidrowRandomizer (), score, 5000, 0.1, 0.25);
```

To use the **TrainingSetScore** object with simulated annealing, simply pass it to the simulated annealing constructor, as was done above.

6.5   Summary

This chapter explained how to use genetic algorithms and simulated annealing to train a neural network. Both of these techniques can use a scoring object, rather than training sets. However, both algorithms can also use a training set if desired.

Genetic algorithms attempt to simulate Darwinian evolution. Neural networks are sorted based on fitness. Better neural networks are allowed to breed;

inferior networks die. The next generation takes genetic material from the fittest neural networks.

Simulated annealing simulates the metallurgical process of annealing. The network weights are taken from a high temperature to a low. As the temperature is lowered, the best networks are chosen. This produces a neural network that is suited to getting better scores.

So far, this book has only discussed how to use a feedforward neural network. This network was trained using propagation training, simulated annealing or a genetic algorithm. Feedforward neural networks are the most commonly seen neural network types. Just because they are the most common, this does not mean they are always the best solution. In the next chapter, we will look at some other neural network architectures.

Chapter 7

Other Neural Network Types

- Understanding the Elman Neural Network

- Understanding the Jordan Neural Network

- The ART1 Neural Network

- Evolving with NEAT

We have primarily looked at feedforward neural networks so far in this book. All connections in a neural network do not need to be forward. It is also possible to create recurrent connections. This chapter will introduce neural networks that are allowed to form recurrent connections.

Though not a recurrent neural network, we will also look at the ART1 neural network. This network type is interesting because it does not have a distinct learning phase like most other neural networks. The ART1 neural network learns as it recognizes patterns. In this way it is always learning, much like the human brain.

This chapter will begin by looking at Elman and Jordan neural networks. These networks are often called simple recurrent neural networks (SRN).

7.1   The Elman Neural Network

Elman and Jordan neural networks are recurrent neural networks that have additional layers and function very similarly to the feedforward networks in previous chapters. They use training techniques similar to feedforward neural networks as well.

Figure 7.1 shows an Elman neural network.

Figure 7.1: The Elman Neural Network

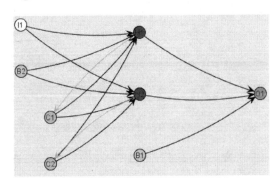

As shown, the Elman neural network uses context neurons. They are labeled as **C1** and **C2**. The context neurons allow feedback. Feedback is when the output from a previous iteration is used as the input for successive iterations. Notice that the context neurons are fed from hidden neuron output. There are no weights on these connections. They are simply an output conduit from hidden neurons to context neurons. The context neurons remember this output and then feed it back to the hidden neurons on the next iteration. Therefore, the context layer is always feeding the hidden layer its own output from the previous iteration.

The connection from the context layer to the hidden layer is weighted. This synapse will learn as the network is trained. Context layers allow a neural network to recognize context.

To see how important context is to a neural network, consider how the previous networks were trained. The order of the training set elements did not really matter. The training set could be jumbled in any way needed and the network would still train in the same manner. With an Elman or a Jordan neural network, the order becomes very important. The training set element previously supported is still affecting the neural network. This becomes very important for predictive neural networks and makes Elman neural networks very useful for temporal neural networks.

Chapter 8 will delve more into temporal neural networks. Temporal networks attempt to see trends in data and predict future data values. Feedforward networks can also be used for prediction, but the input neurons are structured differently. This chapter will focus on how neurons are structured for simple recurrent neural networks.

Dr. Jeffrey Elman created the Elman neural network. Dr. Elman used an XOR pattern to test his neural network. However, he did not use a typical XOR pattern like we've seen in previous chapters. He used a XOR pattern collapsed to just one input neuron. Consider the following XOR truth table.

```
1.0 XOR 0.0 = 1.0
0.0 XOR 0.0 = 0.0
0.0 XOR 1.0 = 1.0
1.0 XOR 1.0 = 0.0
```

Now, collapse this to a string of numbers. To do this simply read the numbers left-to-right, line-by-line. This produces the following:

```
1.0, 0.0, 1.0, 0.0, 0.0, 0.0, 0.0, 1.0, 1.0, 1.0, 1.0, 0.0
```

We will create a neural network that accepts one number from the above list and should predict the next number. This same data will be used with a Jordan neural network later in this chapter. Sample input to this neural network would be as follows:

```
Input Neurons: 1.0 ==> Output Neurons: 0.0
Input Neurons: 0.0 ==> Output Neurons: 1.0
Input Neurons: 1.0 ==> Output Neurons: 0.0
Input Neurons: 0.0 ==> Output Neurons: 0.0
Input Neurons: 0.0 ==> Output Neurons: 0.0
Input Neurons: 0.0 ==> Output Neurons: 0.0
```

It would be impossible to train a typical feedforward neural network for this. The training information would be contradictory. Sometimes an input of 0 results in a 1; other times it results in a 0. An input of 1 has similar issues.

The neural network needs context; it should look at what comes before. We will review an example that uses an Elman and a feedforward network to attempt to predict the output. An example of the Elman neural network can be found at the following location.

```
org.encog.examples.neural.recurrant.elman.ElmanXOR
```

When run, this program produces the following output:

```
Training Elman, Epoch #0 Error:0.32599411611972673
Training Elman, Epoch #1 Error:0.3259917385997097
Training Elman, Epoch #2 Error:0.32598936110238147
Training Elman, Epoch #3 Error:0.32598698362774564
Training Elman, Epoch #4 Error:0.32598460617580305
Training Elman, Epoch #6287 Error:0.08194924225166297
Training Elman, Epoch #6288 Error:0.08194874110333253
Training Elman, Epoch #6289 Error:0.08194824008016807
Training Elman, Epoch #6290 Error:0.08194773918212342

...

Training Elman, Epoch #7953 Error:0.0714145283312322
Training Elman, Epoch #7954 Error:0.0714145283312322
Training Elman, Epoch #7955 Error:0.0714145283312322
Training Elman, Epoch #7956 Error:0.0714145283312322
Training Elman, Epoch #7957 Error:0.0714145283312322
Training Elman, Epoch #7958 Error:0.0714145283312322
Training Elman, Epoch #7959 Error:0.0714145283312322
Training Elman, Epoch #7960 Error:0.0714145283312322
Training Feedforward, Epoch #0 Error:0.32599411611972673
Training Feedforward, Epoch #1 Error:0.3259917385997097
Training Feedforward, Epoch #2 Error:0.32598936110238147
Training Feedforward, Epoch #3 Error:0.32598698362774564
Training Feedforward, Epoch #4 Error:0.32598460617580305

...

Training Feedforward, Epoch #109 Error:0.25000012191064686
Training Feedforward, Epoch #110 Error:0.25000012190802173
Training Feedforward, Epoch #111 Error:0.2500001219053976
Training Feedforward, Epoch #112 Error:0.25000012190277315
Training Feedforward, Epoch #113 Error:0.2500001219001487
Best error rate with Elman Network: 0.0714145283312322
Best error rate with Feedforward Network: 0.2500001219001487
Elman should be able to get into the 10% range,
feedforward should not go below 25%.
The recurrent Elment net can learn better in this case.
```

> If your results are not as good, **try** rerunning, or perhaps training longer.

As you can see, the program attempts to train both a feedforward and an Elman neural network with the temporal XOR data. The feedforward neural network does not learn the data well, but the Elman learns better. In this case, feedforward neural network gets to 49.9% and Elman neural network gets to 7%. The context layer helps considerably.

This program uses random weights to initialize the neural network. If the first run does not produce good results, try rerunning. A better set of starting weights can help.

7.1.1   Creating an Elman Neural Network

Calling the **createElmanNetwork** method creates the Elman neural network in this example. This method is shown here.

```
static BasicNetwork createElmanNetwork() {
  // construct an Elman type network
  ElmanPattern pattern = new ElmanPattern();
  pattern.setActivationFunction(new ActivationSigmoid());
  pattern.setInputNeurons(1);
  pattern.addHiddenLayer(6);
  pattern.setOutputNeurons(1);
  return (BasicNetwork)pattern.generate();
}
```

As you can see from the above code, the **ElmanPattern** is used to actually create the Elman neural network. This provides a quick way to construct an Elman neural network.

7.1.2   Training an Elman Neural Network

Elman neural networks tend to be particularly susceptible to local minima. A local minimum is a point where training stagnates. Visualize the weight matrix and thresholds as a landscape with mountains and valleys. To get to the lowest error, you want to find the lowest valley. Sometimes training finds

a low valley and searches near this valley for a lower spot. It may fail to find
an even lower valley several miles away.

This example's training uses several training strategies to help avoid this
situation. The training code for this example is shown below. The same
training routine is used for both the feedforward and Elman networks and
uses backpropagation with a very small learning rate. However, adding a few
training strategies helps greatly. The **trainNetwork** method is used to train
the neural network. This method is shown here.

```
public static double trainNetwork(final String what,
    final BasicNetwork network, final MLDataSet trainingSet) {
```

One of the strategies employed by this program is a **HybridStrategy**. This
allows an alternative training technique to be used if the main training technique stagnates. We will use simulated annealing as the alternative training
strategy.

```
CalculateScore score = new TrainingSetScore(trainingSet);
final Train trainAlt = new NeuralSimulatedAnnealing(
    network, score, 10, 2, 100);
```

As you can see, we use a training set-based scoring object. For more information about simulated annealing, refer to Chapter 6, "More Supervised
Training." The primary training technique is back propagation.

```
final MLTrain trainMain = new Backpropagation(network, trainingSet
    ,0.000001, 0.0);
```

We will use a **StopTrainingStrategy** to tell us when to stop training. The
StopTrainingStrategy will stop the training when the error rate stagnates.
By default, stagnation is defined as less than a 0.00001% improvement over
100 iterations.

```
final StopTrainingStrategy stop = new StopTrainingStrategy();
```

These strategies are added to the main training technique.

```
trainMain.addStrategy(new Greedy());
trainMain.addStrategy(new HybridStrategy(trainAlt));
trainMain.addStrategy(stop);
```

We also make use of a greedy strategy. This strategy will only allow iterations to improve the error rate of the neural network.

```
int epoch = 0;
while (!stop.shouldStop()) {
  trainMain.iteration();
System.out.println("Training " + what + ", Epoch #" + epoch
  + " Error:" + trainMain.getError());
epoch++;
}
return trainMain.getError();
}
```

The loop continues until the stop strategy indicates that it is time to stop.

7.2   The Jordan Neural Network

Encog also contains a pattern for a Jordan neural network. The Jordan neural network is very similar to the Elman neural network. Figure 7.2 shows a Jordan neural network.

Figure 7.2: The Jordan Neural Network

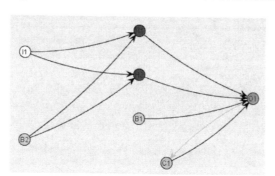

As you can see, a context neuron is used and is labeled **C1**, similar to the Elman network. However, the output from the output layer is fed back to the context layer, rather than the hidden layer. This small change in the architecture can make the Jordan neural network better for certain temporal prediction tasks.

The Jordan neural network has the same number of context neurons as it does output neurons. This is because the context neurons are fed from the output neurons. The XOR operator has only output neuron. This leaves you with a single context neuron when using the Jordan neural network for XOR. Jordan networks work better with a larger number of output neurons.

To construct a Jordan neural network, the **JordanPattern** should be used. The following code demonstrates this.

```
JordanPattern pattern = new JordanPattern();
pattern.setActivationFunction(new ActivationSigmoid());
pattern.setInputNeurons(1);
pattern.addHiddenLayer(6);
pattern.setOutputNeurons(1);
return (BasicNetwork)pattern.generate();
```

The above code would create a Jordan neural network similar to Figure 7.2.

Encog includes an example XOR network that uses the Jordan neural network. This example is included mainly for completeness for comparison of Elman and Jordan on the XOR operator. As previously mentioned, Jordan tends to do better when there are a larger number of output neurons. The Encog XOR example for Jordan will not be able to train to a very low error rate and does not perform noticeably better than a feedforward neural network. The Jordan example can be found at the following location.

```
org.encog.examples.neural.recurrent.jordan.JordanXOR
```

When executed, the above example will compare a feedforward to a Jordan, in similar fashion as the previous example.

7.3 The ART1 Neural Network

The ART1 neural network is a type of Adaptive Resonance Theory (ART) neural network. ART1, developed by Stephen Grossberg and Gail Carpenter, supports only bipolar input. The ART1 neural network is trained as it is used and is used for classification. New patterns are presented to the ART1 network and are classified into either new or existing classes. Once the maximum number of classes has been used, the network will report that it is out of classes.

An ART1 network appears as a simple two-layer neural network. However, unlike a feedforward neural network, there are weights in both directions between the input and output layers. The input neurons are used to present patterns to the ART1 network. ART1 uses bipolar numbers, so each input neuron is either on or off. A value of one represents on, and a value of negative one represents off.

The output neurons define the groups that the ART1 neural network will recognize. Each output neuron represents one group.

7.3.1 Using the ART1 Neural Network

We will now see how to actually make use of an ART1 network. The example presented here will create a network that is given a series of patterns to learn to recognize. This example can be found at the following location.

```
org.encog.examples.neural.art.art1.NeuralART1
```

This example constructs an ART1 network. This network will be presented new patterns to recognize and learn. If a new pattern is similar to a previous pattern, then the new pattern is identified as belonging to the same group as the original pattern. If the pattern is not similar to a previous pattern, then a new group is created. If there is already one group per output neuron, then the neural network reports that it can learn no more patterns.

The output from this example can be seen here.

```
   O  - 0
 O O  - 1
   O  - 1
 O O  - 2
   O  - 1
 O O  - 2
   O  - 1
OO O  - 3
OO    - 3
OO O  - 4
OO    - 3
```

```
OOO    — 5
OO     — 5
O      — 5
OO     — 6
OOO    — 7
OOOO   — 8
OOOOO  — 9
O      — 5
  O    — 3
   O   — 2
    O  — 0
     O — 1
    O O — 4
  OO O  — 9
  OO   — 7
OOO    — 8
OO     — 6
OOOO   — new Input and all Classes exhausted
OOOOO  — new Input and all Classes exhausted
```

The above output shows that the neural network is presented with patterns. The number to the right indicates in which group the ART1 network placed the pattern. Some patterns are grouped with previous patterns while other patterns form new groups. Once all of the output neurons have been assigned to a group, the neural network can learn no more patterns. Once this happens, the network reports that all classes have been exhausted.

First, an ART1 neural network must be created. This can be done with the following code.

```
ART1 logic = new ART1(INPUT_NEURONS,OUTPUT_NEURONS);
```

This creates a new ART1 network with the specified number of input neurons and output neurons. Here we create a neural network with 5 input neurons and 10 output neurons. This neural network will be capable of clustering input into 10 clusters.

Because the input patterns are stored as string arrays, they must be converted to a **boolean** array that can be presented to the neural network. Because the ART1 network is bipolar, it only accepts Boolean values. The following code converts each of the pattern strings into an array of Boolean values.

```
public void setupInput () {
  this.input = new boolean[PATTERN.length][INPUT_NEURONS];
  for (int n = 0; n < PATTERN.length; n++) {
    for (int i = 0; i < INPUT_NEURONS; i++) {
      this.input[n][i] = (PATTERN[n].charAt(i) == 'O');
    }
  }
}
```

The patterns are stored in the **PATTERN** array. The converted patterns will be stored in the **boolean input** array.

Now that a **boolean** array represents the input patterns, we can present each pattern to the neural network to be clustered. This is done with the following code, beginning by looping through each of the patterns:

```
for (int i = 0; i < PATTERN.length; i++) {
```

First, we create a **BiPolarNeuralData** object that will hold the input pattern. A second object is created to hold the output from the neural network.

```
BiPolarNeuralData in = new BiPolarNeuralData(this.input[i]);
BiPolarNeuralData out = new BiPolarNeuralData(OUTPUT_NEURONS);
```

Using the input, we compute the output.

```
logic.compute(in, out);
```

Determine if there is a winning output neuron. If there is, this is the cluster that the input belongs to.

```
if (logic.hasWinner()) {
  System.out.println(PATTERN[i] + " - " + logic.getWinner());
} else {
```

If there is no winning neuron, the user is informed that all classes have been used.

```
  System.out.println(PATTERN[i]
      + " - new Input and all Classes exhausted");
  }
}
```

The ART1 is a network that can be used to cluster data on the fly. There is no distinct learning phase; it will cluster data as it is received.

7.4   The NEAT Neural Network

NeuroEvolution of Augmenting Topologies (NEAT) is a Genetic Algorithm for evolving the structure and weights of a neural network. NEAT was developed by Ken Stanley at The University of Texas at Austin. NEAT relieves the neural network programmer of the tedious task of figuring out the optimal structure of a neural network's hidden layer.

A NEAT neural network has an input and output layer, just like the more common feedforward neural networks. A NEAT network starts with only an input layer and output layer. The rest is evolved as the training progresses. Connections inside of a NEAT neural network can be feedforward, recurrent, or self-connected. All of these connection types will be tried by NEAT as it attempts to evolve a neural network capable of the given task.

Figure 7.3: An NEAT Network before Evolving

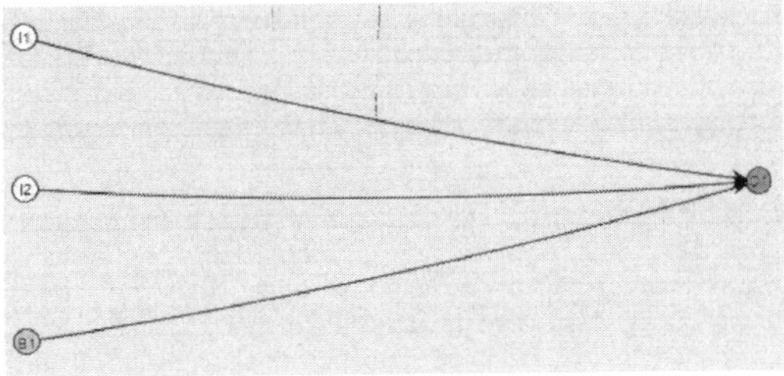

As you can see, the above network has only an input and hidden layers. This is not sufficient to learn XOR. These networks evolve by adding neurons and connections. Figure 7.4 shows a neural network that has evolved to process the XOR operator.

Figure 7.4: An NEAT Network after Evolving

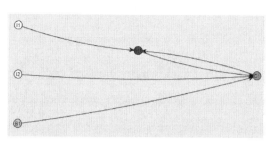

The above network evolved from the previous network. An additional hidden neuron was added between the first input neuron and the output neuron. Additionally, a recurrent connection was made from the output neuron back to the first hidden neuron. These minor additions allow the neural network to learn the XOR operator. The connections and neurons are not the only things being evolved. The weights between these neurons were evolved as well.

As shown in Figure 7.4, a NEAT network does not have clearly defined layers like traditional feed forward networks. There is a hidden neuron, but not really a hidden layer. If this were a traditional hidden layer, both input neurons would be connected to the hidden neuron.

NEAT is a complex neural network type and training method. Additionally, there is a new version of NEAT, called HyperNEAT. Complete coverage of NEAT is beyond the scope of this book. I will likely release a future book on focused on Encog application of NEAT and HyperNEAT. This section will focus on how to use NEAT as a potential replacement for a feedforward neural network, providing you all of the critical information for using NEAT with Encog.

7.4.1 Creating an Encog NEAT Population

This section will show how to use a NEAT network to learn the XOR operator. There is very little difference between the code in this example that used for a feedforward neural network to learn the XOR operator. One of Encog's core objectives is to make machine learning methods as interchangeable as possible.

You can see this example at the following location.

```
org.encog.examples.neural.xor.XORNEAT
```

This example begins by creating an XOR training set to provide the XOR inputs and expected outputs to the neural network. To review the expected inputs and outputs for the XOR operator, refer to Chapter 3.

```
MLDataSet trainingSet = new BasicMLDataSet(XOR_INPUT, XOR_IDEAL);
```

Next a NEAT population is created. Previously, we would create a single neural network to be trained. NEAT requires the creation of an entire population of networks. This population will go through generations producing better neural networks. Only the fit members of the population will be allowed to breed new neural networks.

```
NEATPopulation pop = new NEATPopulation(2,1,1000);
```

The above population is created with two input neurons, one output neuron and a population size of 1,000. The larger the population, the better the networks will train. However, larger populations will run slower and consume more memory.

Earlier we said that only the fit members of the population are allowed to breed to create the next generations.

```
CalculateScore score = new TrainingSetScore(trainingSet);
```

One final required step is to set an output activation function for the NEAT network. This is different than the "NEAT activation function," which is usually sigmoid or TANH. Rather, this activation function is applied to all data being read from the neural network.

Treat any output from neural network below 0.5 as zero, and any above as one. This can be done with a step activation function, as follows.

```
ActivationStep step = new ActivationStep();
step.setCenter(0.5);
pop.setOutputActivationFunction(step);
```

Now that the population has been created, it must be trained.

7.4.2 Training an Encog NEAT Neural Network

Training a NEAT neural network is very similar to training any other neural network in Encog: create a training object and begin looping through iterations. As these iterations progress, the quality of the neural networks in the population should increase.

A NEAT neural network is trained with the **NEATTraining** class. Here you can see a **NEATTraining** object being created.

```
final NEATTraining train = new NEATTraining(score,pop);
```

This object trains the population to a 1% error rate.

```
EncogUtility.trainToError(train, 0.01);
```

Once the population has been trained, extract the best neural network.

```
NEATNetwork network = (NEATNetwork)train.getMethod();
```

With an established neural network, its performance must be tested. First, clear out any recurrent layers from previous runs.

```
network.clearContext();
```

Now, display the results from the neural network.

```
System.out.println("Neural Network Results:");
EncogUtility.evaluate(network, trainingSet);
```

This will produce the following output.

```
Beginning training...
Iteration #1 Error:25.000000% Target Error: 1.000000%
Iteration #2 Error:0.000000% Target Error: 1.000000%
Neural Network Results:
Input=0.0000,0.0000, Actual=0.0000, Ideal=0.0000
Input=1.0000,0.0000, Actual=1.0000, Ideal=1.0000
Input=0.0000,1.0000, Actual=1.0000, Ideal=1.0000
Input=1.0000,1.0000, Actual=0.0000, Ideal=0.0000
```

The neural network only took two iterations to produce a neural network that knew how to function as an XOR operator. The network has learned the XOR operator from the above results. XOR will produce an output of 1.0 only when the two inputs are not both of the same value.

7.5   Summary

While previous chapters focused mainly on feedforward neural networks, this chapter explores some of the other Encog-supported network types including the Elman, Jordan, ART1 and NEAT neural networks.

In this chapter you learned about recurrent neural networks, which contain connections backwards to previous layers. Elman and Jordan neural networks make use of a context layer. This context layer allows them to learn patterns that span several items of training data. This makes them very useful for temporal neural networks.

The ART1 neural network can be used to learn binary patterns. Unlike other neural networks, there is no distinct learning and usage state. The ART1 neural network learns as it is used and requires no training stage. This mimics the human brain in that humans learn a task as they perform that task.

This chapter concluded with the NEAT neural network. The NEAT network does not have hidden layers like a typical feedforward neural network. A NEAT network starts out with only an input and output layer. The structure of the hidden neurons evolves as the NEAT network is trained using a genetic algorithm.

In the next chapter we will look at temporal neural networks. A temporal neural network is used to attempt to predict the future. This type of neural network can be very useful in a variety of fields such as finance, signal processing and general business. The next chapter will show how to structure input data for neural network queries to make a future prediction.

Chapter 8

Using Temporal Data

- How a Predictive Neural Network Works

- Using the Encog Temporal Dataset

- Attempting to Predict Sunspots

- Using the Encog Market Dataset

- Attempting to Predict the Stock Market

Prediction is another common use for neural networks. A predictive neural network will attempt to predict future values based on present and past values. Such neural networks are called temporal neural networks because they operate over time. This chapter will introduce temporal neural networks and the support classes that Encog provides for them.

In this chapter, you will see two applications of Encog temporal neural networks. First, we will look at how to use Encog to predict sunspots. Sunspots are reasonably predictable and the neural network should be able to learn future patterns by analyzing past data. Next, we will examine a simple case of applying a neural network to making stock market predictions.

Before we look at either example we must see how a temporal neural network actually works. A temporal neural network is usually either a feedforward or simple recurrent network. Structured properly, the feedforward neural networks shown so far could be structured as a temporal neural network by assigning certain input and output neurons.

8.1   How a Predictive Neural Network Works

A predictive neural network uses its inputs to accept information about current data and uses its outputs to predict future data. It uses two "windows," a future window and a past window. Both windows must have a window size, which is the amount of data that is either predicted or is needed to predict. To see the two windows in action, consider the following data.

```
Day  1:  100
Day  2:  102
Day  3:  104
Day  4:  110
Day  5:  99
Day  6:  100
Day  7:  105
Day  8:  106
Day  9:  110
Day  10:  120
```

Consider a temporal neural network with a past window size of five and a future window size of two. This neural network would have five input neurons and two output neurons. We would break the above data among these windows to produce training data. The following data shows one such element of training data.

```
Input  1:  Day  1:  100  (input  neuron)
Input  2:  Day  2:  102  (input  neuron)
Input  3:  Day  3:  104  (input  neuron)
Input  4:  Day  4:  110  (input  neuron)
Input  5:  Day  5:  99   (input  neuron)
Ideal  1:  Day  6:  100  (output  neuron)
Ideal  2:  Day  7:  105  (output  neuron)
```

Of course the data above needs to be normalized in some way before it can be fed to the neural network. The above illustration simply shows how the input and output neurons are mapped to the actual data. To get additional data, both windows are simply slid forward. The next element of training data would be as follows.

```
Input 1: Day 2: 102 (input neuron)
Input 2: Day 3: 104 (input neuron)
Input 3: Day 4: 110 (input neuron)
Input 4: Day 5: 99  (input neuron)
Input 5: Day 6: 100 (input neuron)
Ideal 1: Day 7: 105 (output neuron)
Ideal 2: Day 8: 106 (output neuron)
```

You would continue sliding the past and future windows forward as you generate more training data. Encog contains specialized classes to prepare data in this format. Simply specify the size of the past, or input, window and the future, or output, window. These specialized classes will be discussed in the next section.

8.2   Using the Encog Temporal Dataset

The Encog temporal dataset is contained in the following package:

```
org.encog.neural.data.temporal
```

There are a total of four classes that make up the Encog temporal dataset. These classes are as follows:

- **TemporalDataDescription**

- **TemporalError**

- **TemporalMLDataSet**

- **TemporalPoint**

The **TemporalDataDescription** class describes one unit of data that is either used for prediction or output. The **TemporalError** class is an exception that is thrown if there is an error while processing the temporal data. The **TemporalMLDataSet** class operates just like any Encog dataset and allows

the temporal data to be used for training. The **TemporalPoint** class represents one point of temporal data.

To begin using a **TemporalMLDataSet** we must instantiate it as follows:

```
TemporalMLDataSet result =
  new TemporalMLDataSet(
    [past window size] , [future window size] );
```

The above instantiation specifies both the size of the past and future windows.
You must also define one or more **TemporalDataDescription** objects. These
define the individual items inside of the past and future windows. One single
TemporalDataDescription object can function as both a past and a future
window element as illustrated in the code below.

```
TemporalDataDescription desc =
  new TemporalDataDescription(
    [calculation type] , [use for past] , [use for future] );
result.addDescription(desc);
```

To specify that a **TemporalDataDescription** object functions as both a past
and future element, use the value **true** for the last two parameters. There are
several calculation types that you can specify for each data description. These
types are summarized here.

- TemporalDataDescription.RAW

- TemporalDataDescription.PERCENT_CHANGE

- TemporalDataDescription.DELTA_CHANGE

The **RAW** type specifies that the data points should be passed on to the
neural network unmodified. The **PERCENT_CHANGE** specifies that each
point should be passed on as a percentage change. The **DELTA_CHANGE**
specifies that each point should be passed on as the actual change between the
two values. If you are normalizing the data yourself, you would use the RAW
type. Otherwise, it is very likely you would use the **PERCENT_CHANGE**
type.

Next, provide the raw data to train the temporal network from. To do this, create **TemporalPoint** objects and add them to the temporal dataset. Each **TemporalPoint** object can contain multiple values, i.e. have the same number of values in each temporal data point as in the **TemporalDataDescription** objects. The following code shows how to define a temporal data point.

```
TemporalPoint  point = new TemporalPoint( [number of values] );
point.setSequence( [a sequence number] );
point.setData(0, [ value 1 ] );
point.setData(1, [ value 2 ] );
result.getPoints().add(point);
```

Every data point should have a sequence number in order to sort the data points. The **setData** method calls allow the individual values to be set and should match the specified number of values in the constructor.

Finally, call the **generate** method. This method takes all of the temporal points and creates the training set. After **generate** has been called, the **TemportalMLDataSet** object can be use for training.

```
result.generate();
```

The next section will use a **TemportalMLDataSet** object to predict sunspots.

8.3 Application to Sunspots

In this section we will see how to use Encog to predict sunspots, which are fairly periodic and predictable. A neural network can learn this pattern and predict the number of sunspots with reasonable accuracy. The output from the sunspot prediction program is shown below. Of course, the neural network first begins training and will train until the error rate falls below six percent.

```
Epoch #1 Error:0.39165411390480664
Epoch #2 Error:1.2907898518116008
Epoch #3 Error:1.275679853982214
Epoch #4 Error:0.8026954615095163
```

```
Epoch #5 Error:0.4999305514145095
Epoch #6 Error:0.468223450164209
Epoch #7 Error:0.22034289938540677
Epoch #8 Error:0.2406776630699879

...

Epoch #128 Error:0.06025613803011326
Epoch #129 Error:0.06002069579351901
Epoch #130 Error:0.059830227113598734
YearActualPredictClosed Loop Predict
19600.57230.55470.5547
19610.32670.40750.3918
19620.25770.18370.2672
19630.21730.11900.0739
19640.14290.17380.1135
19650.16350.26310.3650
19660.29770.23270.4203
19670.49460.28700.1342
19680.54550.61670.3533
19690.54380.51110.6415
19700.53950.38300.4011
19710.38010.40720.2469
19720.38980.21480.2342
19730.25980.25330.1788
19740.24510.16860.2163
19750.16520.19680.2064
19760.15300.14700.2032
19770.21480.15330.1751
19780.48910.35790.1014
```

Once the network has been trained, it tries to predict the number of sunspots between 1960 and 1978. It does this with at least some degree of accuracy. The number displayed is normalized and simply provides an idea of the relative number of sunspots. A larger number indicates more sunspot activity; a lower number indicates less sunspot activity.

There are two prediction numbers given: the regular prediction and the closed-loop prediction. Both prediction types use a past window of 30 and a future window of 1. The regular prediction simply uses the last 30 values from real data. The closed loop starts this way and, as it proceeds, its own predictions become the input as the window slides forward. This usually results in a less accurate prediction because any mistakes the neural network makes are compounded.

We will now examine how this program was implemented. This program can be found at the following location.

```
org.encog.examples.neural.predict.sunspot.PredictSunspot
```

As you can see, the program has sunspot data hardcoded near the top of the file. This data was taken from a C-based neural network example program. You can find the original application at the following URL:

http://www.neural-networks-at-your-fingertips.com/bpn.html

The older, C-based neural network example was modified to make use of Encog. You will notice that the Encog version is much shorter than the C-based version. This is because much of what the example did was already implemented in Encog. Further, the Encog version trains the network faster because it makes use of resilient propagation, whereas the C-based example makes use of backpropagation.

This example goes through a two-step process for using the data. First, the raw data is normalized. Then, this normalized data is loaded into a **TemporalMLDataSet** object for temporal training. The **normalizeSunspots** method is called to normalize the sunspots. This method is shown below.

```
public void normalizeSunspots(double lo, double hi) {
```

The **hi** and **lo** parameters specify the high and low range to which the sunspots should be normalized. This specifies the normalized sunspot range. Normalization was discussed in Chapter 2. For this example, the **lo** value is 0.1 and the **high** value is 0.9.

To normalize these arrays, create an instance of the **NormalizeArray** class. This object will allow you to quickly normalize an array. To use this object, simply set the normalized high and low values, as follows.

```
NormalizeArray norm = new NormalizeArray();
norm.setNormalizedHigh( hi);
norm.setNormalizedLow( lo);
```

The array can now be normalized to this range by calling the **process** method.

```
normalizedSunspots = norm.process(SUNSPOTS);
```

Now copy the normalized sunspots to the closed loop sunspots.

```
closedLoopSunspots = EngineArray.arrayCopy(normalizedSunspots);
```

Initially, the closed-loop array starts out the same as the regular prediction. However, its predictions will used to fill this array.

Now that the sunspot data has been normalized, it should be converted to temporal data. This is done by calling the **generateTraining** method, shown below.

```
public MLDataSet generateTraining()
{
```

This method will return an Encog dataset that can be used for training. First a **TemporalMLDataSet** is created and past and future window sizes are specified.

```
TemporalMLDataSet result = new TemporalMLDataSet(WINDOW_SIZE, 1);
```

We will have a single data description. Because the data is already normalized, we will use RAW data. This data description will be used for both input and prediction, as the last two parameters specify. Finally, we add this description to the dataset.

```
TemporalDataDescription desc = new TemporalDataDescription(
    TemporalDataDescription.Type.RAW, true, true);
result.addDescription(desc);
```

It is now necessary to create all of the data points. We will loop between the starting and ending year, which are the years used to train the neural network. Other years will be used to test the neural network's predictive ability.

```
for(int year = TRAIN_START; year<TRAIN_END; year++)
{
```

Each data point will have only one value to predict the sunspots. The sequence is the year, because there is only one sunspot sample per year.

```
TemporalPoint point = new TemporalPoint(1);
point.setSequence(year);
```

The one value we are using is the normalized number of sunspots. This number is both what we use to predict from past values and what we hope to predict in the future.

```
        point.setData(0, this.normalizedSunspots[year]);
        result.getPoints().add(point);
}
```

Finally, we generate the training set and return it.

```
    result.generate();
    return result;
}
```

The data is now ready for training. This dataset is trained using resilient propagation. This process is the same as those used many times earlier in this book. Once training is complete, we will attempt to predict sunspots using the application. This is done with the **predict** method, which is shown here.

```
public void predict(BasicNetwork network)
{
```

First, we create a **NumberFormat** object so that the numbers can be properly formatted. We will display four decimal places.

```
NumberFormat f = NumberFormat.getNumberInstance();
f.setMaximumFractionDigits(4);
f.setMinimumFractionDigits(4);
```

We display the heading for the table and begin to loop through the evaluation years.

```
System.out.println("Year\tActual\tPredict\tClosed Loop Predict")
    ;
for(int year=EVALUATE_START;year<EVALUATE_END;year++)
{
```

We create input into the neural network based on actual data, which will be the actual prediction. We extract 30 years worth of data for the past window.

```
MLData input = new BasicMLData(WINDOW_SIZE);
for(int i=0;i<input.size();i++)
{
  input.setData(i,this.normalizedSunspots[
    (year-WINDOW_SIZE)+i]);
}
```

The neural network is presented with the data and we retrieve the prediction.

```
MLData output = network.compute(input);
double prediction = output.getData(0);
```

The prediction is saved to the closed-loop array for use with future predictions.

```
this.closedLoopSunspots[year] = prediction;
```

We will now calculate the closed-loop value. The calculation is essentially the same except that the closed-loop data, which is continually modified, is used. Just as before, we use 30 years worth of data.

```
for(int i=0;i<input.size();i++)
{
  input.setData(i,this.closedLoopSunspots[
    (year-WINDOW_SIZE)+i]);
}
```

We compute the output.

```
output = network.compute(input);
double closedLoopPrediction = output.getData(0);
```

Finally, we display the closed-loop prediction, the regular prediction and the actual value.

```
System.out.println((STARTING_YEAR+year)
  +"\t"+f.format(this.normalizedSunspots[year])
  +"\t"+f.format(prediction)+"\t"+f.format(
    closedLoopPrediction));
  }
}
```

This will display a list of all of the sunspot predictions made by Encog. In the next section we will see how Encog can automatically pull current market information and attempt to predict stock market directions.

8.4   Using the Encog Market Dataset

Encog also includes a dataset specifically designed for stock market data. This dataset is capable of downloading data from external sources. Currently, the only external source included in Encog is Yahoo Finance. The Encog market dataset is built on top of the temporal dataset and most classes in the Encog market dataset descend directly from corresponding classes in the temporal data set.

The following classes make up the Encog Market Dataset package:

- **MarketDataDescription**

- **MarketDataType**

- **MarketError**

- **MarketMLDataSet**

- **MarketPoint**

- **TickerSymbol**

The **MarketDataDescription** class represents one piece of market data that is part of either the past or future window. It descends from the **Temporal-DataDescription** class. It consists primarily of a **TickerSymbol** object and a **MarketDataType** enumeration. The ticker symbol specifies the security to include and the **MarketDataType** specifies what type of data from this security to use. The available data types are listed below.

- **OPEN** - The market open for the day.

- **CLOSE** - The market close for the day.

- **VOLUME** - The volume for the day.

- **ADJUSTED_CLOSE** - The adjusted close. Adjusted for splits and dividends.

- **HIGH** - The high for the day.

- **LOW** - The low for the day.

These are the market data types criteria currently supported by Encog. They are all represented inside of the **MarketDataType** enumeration.

The **MarketMLDataSet** class is descended from the **TemporalML-DataSet**. This is the main class when creating market-based training data for Encog. This class is an Encog dataset and can be trained. If any errors occur, the **MarketError** exception will be thrown.

The **MarketPoint** class descends from the **TemporalPoint**. You will usually not deal with this object directly, as Encog usually downloads market data from Yahoo Finance. The following code shows the general format for using the **MarketMLDataSet** class. First, create a loader. Currently, the **YahooFinanceLoader** is the only public loader available for Encog.

```
MarketLoader loader = new YahooFinanceLoader();
```

Next, we create the market dataset. We pass the loader, as well as the size of the past and future windows.

```
MarketMLDataSet market = new MarketMLDataSet(
loader,
[past window size],
[future window size] );
```

Next create a **MarketDataDescription** object. To do this, specify the needed ticker symbol and data type. The last two true values at the end specify that this item is used both for past and predictive purposes.

```
final MarketDataDescription desc = new MarketDataDescription(
[ticker], [data type needed] , true, true);
```

We add this data description to the dataset.

```
market.addDescription(desc);
```

We can add additional descriptions as needed. Next, load the market data and generate the training data.

```
market.load( [begin date], [end date] );
market.generate();
```

As shown in the code, the beginning and ending dates must be specified. This tells Encog the range from which to generate training data.

8.5   Application to the Stock Market

We will now look at an example of applying Encog to stock market prediction. This program attempts to predict the direction of a single stock based on past performance. This is a very simple stock market example and is not meant to offer any sort of investment advice.

First, let's explain how to run this example. There are four distinct modes in which this example can be run, depending on the command line argument that was passed. These arguments are summarized below.

- **generate** - Download financial data and generate training file.

- **train** - Train the neural network.

- **evaluate** - Evaluate the neural network.

- **prune** - Evaluate try a number of different architectures to determine the best configuration.

To begin the example you should run the main class, which is named **Market-Predict**. The following sections will show how this example generates data, trains and then evaluates the resulting neural network. This application is located at the following location.

```
org.encog.examples.neural.predict.market.MarketPredict
```

Each of these modes to use this program will now be covered.

8.5.1   Generating Training Data

The first step is to generate the training data. The example is going to download about eight years worth of financial information to train with. It takes some time to download and process this information. The data is downloaded and written to an Encog EG file. The class **MarketBuildTraining** provides this functionality.

All work performed by this class is in the **static** method named **generate**. This method is shown below.

```
public static void generate(File dataDir) {
```

This method begins by creating a **YahooFinanceLoader** that will load the requested financial data.

```
final MarketLoader loader = new YahooFinanceLoader();
```

A new **MarketMLDataSet** object is created that will use the **loader** and a specified size for the past and future windows. By default, the program uses a future window size of one and a past window size of 10. These constants are all defined in the **Config** class. This is the way to control how the network is structured and trained by changing any of the values in the **Config** class.

```
final MarketMLDataSet market = new MarketMLDataSet(loader,
    Config.INPUT_WINDOW, Config.PREDICT_WINDOW);
```

The program uses a single market value from which to make predictions. It will use the adjusted closing price of the specified security. The security that the program is trying to predict is specified in the **Config** class.

```
final MarketDataDescription desc = new MarketDataDescription(
    Config.TICKER, MarketDataType.ADJUSTED_CLOSE, true, true);
market.addDescription(desc);
```

The market data is now loaded beginning two years ago and ending two months prior to today. The last two months will be used to evaluate the neural network's performance.

```
Calendar end = new GregorianCalendar();// end today
Calendar begin = (Calendar) end.clone();// begin 30 days ago
begin.add(Calendar.DATE, -60);
```

```
end.add(Calendar.DATE, -60);
begin.add(Calendar.YEAR, -2);
market.load(begin.getTime(), end.getTime());
market.generate();
```

We now save the training data to a binary **EGB** file. It is important to note that **TemporalDataSet** or any of its derived classes will persist raw numeric data, just as a **BasicMLDataSet** would. Only the generated data will be saved, not the other support objects such as the **MarketDataDescription** objects.

```
EncogUtility.saveEGB(new File(
    dataDir, Config.TRAINING_FILE), market);
```

We will create a network to save to an EG file. This network is a simple feedforward neural network that may have one or two hidden layers. The sizes of the hidden layers are specified in the **Config** class.

```
final BasicNetwork network = EncogUtility.simpleFeedForward(
    market.getInputSize(),
    Config.HIDDEN1_COUNT,
    Config.HIDDEN2_COUNT,
    market.getIdealSize(),
    true);
```

We now create the **EG** file and store the network to an EG file.

```
EncogDirectoryPersistence.saveObject(
    new File(dataDir, Config.NETWORK_FILE), network);
}
```

Later phases of the program, such as the training and evaluation phases, will use this file.

8.5.2 Training the Neural Network

Training the neural network is very simple. The network and training data are already created and stored in an EG file. All that the training class needs to do is load both of these resources from the EG file and begin training. The **MarketTrain** class does this.

The **static** method **train** performs all of the training. This method is shown here.

```
public static void train() {
```

The method begins by verifying whether the Encog EG file is present. Training data and the network will be loaded from here.

```
final File networkFile = new File(dataDir, Config.NETWORK_FILE);
final File trainingFile = new File(dataDir, Config.TRAINING_FILE);
// network file
if (!networkFile.exists()) {
  System.out.println("Can't read file: "
    + networkFile.getAbsolutePath());
  return;
}
```

Next, use the **EncogDirectoryPersistence** object to load the EG file. We will extract a network.

```
BasicNetwork network = (BasicNetwork)EncogDirectoryPersistence.
    loadObject(networkFile);
```

Next, load the training file from disk. This network will be used for training.

```
// training file
if (!trainingFile.exists()) {
  System.out.println("Can't read file: " + trainingFile.
      getAbsolutePath());
  return;
}
final MLDataSet trainingSet = EncogUtility.loadEGB2Memory(
    trainingFile);
```

The neural network is now ready to train. We will use **EncogUtility** training and loop for the number of minutes specified in the **Config** class. This is the same as creating a training object and using iterations, as was done previously in this book. The **trainConsole** method is simply a shortcut to run the iterations for a specified number of minutes.

```
// train the neural network
EncogUtility.trainConsole(network, trainingSet, Config.
    TRAINING_MINUTES);
```

Finally, the neural network is saved back to the EG file.

```
System.out.println("Final Error: " + network.calculateError(
    trainingSet));
System.out.println("Training complete, saving network.");
EncogDirectoryPersistence.saveObject(networkFile, network);
System.out.println("Network saved.");
Encog.getInstance().shutdown();
```

At this point, the neural network is trained. To further train the neural network, run the training again or move on to evaluating the neural network. If you train the same neural network again using resilient propagation, the error rate will initially spike. This is because the resilient propagation algorithm must reestablish proper delta values for training.

8.5.3   Incremental Pruning

One challenge with neural networks is determining the optimal architecture for the hidden layers. Should there be one hidden layer or two? How many neurons should be in each of the hidden layers? There are no easy answers to these questions.

Generally, it is best to start with a neural network with one hidden layer and double the number of hidden neurons as input neurons. There are some reports that suggest that the second hidden layer has no advantages, although this is often debated. Other reports suggest a second hidden layer can sometimes lead to faster convergence. For more information, see the hidden layer page on the Heaton Research wiki.

http://www.heatonresearch.com/wiki/Hidden_Layers

One utility provided by Encog is the incremental pruning class. This class allows you to use a brute force technique to determine an optimal hidden layer configuration. Calling the market example with the **prune** argument will perform an incremental prune. This will try a number of different hidden layer configurations to attempt to find the best one.

This command begins by loading a training set to memory.

```
MLDataSet training = EncogUtility.loadEGB2Memory(file);
```

Next a pattern is created to specify the type of neural network to be created.

```
FeedForwardPattern pattern = new FeedForwardPattern();
pattern.setInputNeurons(training.getInputSize());
pattern.setOutputNeurons(training.getIdealSize());
pattern.setActivationFunction(new ActivationTANH());
```

The above code specifies the creation of feedforward neural networks using the hyperbolic tangent activation function. Next, the pruning object is created.

```
PruneIncremental prune = new PruneIncremental(training, pattern,
    100, 1, 10, new ConsoleStatusReportable());
```

The object will perform 100 training iterations, try one weight for each, and have 10 top networks. The object will take the 10 best networks after 100 training iterations. The best of these 10 is chosen to be the network with the smallest number of links.

The user may also specify the number and sizes of the hidden layers to try. Each call to **addHiddenLayer** specifies the lower and upper bound to try. The first call to **addHiddenLayer** specifies the range for the first hidden layer. Here we specify to try hidden layer one sizes from 5 to 50. Because the lower point is not zero, we are required to have a first hidden layer.

```
prune.addHiddenLayer(5, 50);
```

Next we specify the size for the second hidden layer. Here we are trying hidden layers between 0 and 50 neurons. Because the low point is zero, we will also try neural networks with no second layer.

```
prune.addHiddenLayer(0, 50);
```

Now that the object has been setup we are ready to search. Calling the **process** method will begin the search.

```
prune.process();
```

Once the search is completed you can call the **getBestNetwork** to get the best performing network. The following code obtains this network and saves it.

```
File networkFile = new File(dataDir, Config.NETWORK_FILE);
EncogDirectoryPersistence.saveObject(networkFile, prune.
    getBestNetwork());
```

We now have a neural network saved with a good combination of hidden layers and neurons. The pruning object does not train each network particularly well, as it is trying to search a large number of networks. At this point, you will want to further train this best network.

8.5.4   Evaluating the Neural Network

We are now ready to evaluate the neural network using the trained neural network from the last section and gauge its performance on actual current stock market data. The **MarketEvaluate** class contains all of the evaluation code.

There are two important methods used during the evaluation process. The first is the **determineDirection** class. We are not attempting to determine the actual percent change for a security, but rather, which direction it will move the next day.

```
public static Direction determineDirection(final double d) {
   if( d<0 )
     return Direction.down;
   else
     return Direction.up;
}
```

This method simply returns an enumeration that specifies whether the stock price moved up or down.

We will need some current market data to evaluate against. The **grabData** method obtains the necessary market data. It makes use of a **MarketML-DataSet**, just as the training does, to obtain some market data. This method is shown here.

```
public static MarketMLDataSet grabData() {
```

Just like the training data generation, market data is loaded from a **Yahoo-FinanceLoader** object.

```
MarketLoader loader = new YahooFinanceLoader();
MarketMLDataSet result = new MarketMLDataSet(
   loader,
   Config.INPUT_WINDOW,
   Config.PREDICT_WINDOW);
```

We create exactly the same data description as was used for training: the adjusted close for the specified ticker symbol. Past and future data are also desired. By feeding past data to the neural network, we will see how well the output matches the future data.

```
MarketDataDescription desc = new MarketDataDescription(
   Config.TICKER,
   MarketDataType.ADJUSTED_CLOSE,
   true,
   true);
result.addDescription(desc);
```

Choose what date range to evaluate the network. We will grab the last 60 days worth of data.

```
Calendar end = new GregorianCalendar();// end today
Calendar begin = (Calendar)end.clone();// begin 60 days ago
begin.add(Calendar.DATE, -60);
```

The market data is now loaded and generated by using the **load** method call.

```
   result.load(begin.getTime(), end.getTime());
   result.generate();
   return result;
}
```

The resulting data is returned to the calling method. Now that we have covered the support methods, it is time to learn how the actual training occurs. The **static** method **evaluate** performs the actual evaluation. This method is shown below.

```
public static void evaluate() {
```

First, make sure that the Encog EG file exists.

```
File file = new File(Config.FILENAME);
if( !file.exists() ) {
  System.out.println("Can't read file: " + file.getAbsolutePath()
      );
  return;
}

  EncogPersistedCollection encog = new EncogPersistedCollection(
      file);
```

Then, we load the neural network from the EG file. Use the neural network that was trained in the previous section.

```
BasicNetwork network = (BasicNetwork)EncogDirectoryPersistence.
    loadObject(file);
```

Load the market data to be used for network evaluation. This is done using the **grabData** method discussed earlier in this section.

```
MarketMLDataSet data = grabData();
```

Use a formatter to format the percentages.

```
DecimalFormat format = new DecimalFormat("#0.0000");
```

During evaluation, count the number of cases examined and how many were correct.

```
int count = 0;
int correct = 0;
```

Loop over all of the loaded market data.

```
for(MLDataPair pair: data) {
```

Retrieve one training pair and obtain the actual data as well as what was predicted. The predicted data is determined by running the network using the **compute** method.

```
MLData input = pair.getInput();
MLData actualData = pair.getIdeal();
MLData predictData = network.compute(input);
```

Now retrieve the actual and predicted data and calculate the difference. This establishes the accuracy off the neural network predicting the actual price change.

```
double actual = actualData.getData(0);
double predict = predictData.getData(0);
double diff = Math.abs(predict-actual);
```

Also calculate the direction the network predicted security takes versus the direction the security actually took.

```
Direction actualDirection = determineDirection(actual);
Direction predictDirection = determineDirection(predict);
```

If the direction was correct, increment the correct count by one. Either way, increment the total count by one.

```
if( actualDirection==predictDirection )
  correct++;
count++;
```

Display the results for each case examined.

```
System.out.println("Day " + count+":actual="
  +format.format(actual)+"("+actualDirection+")"
  +",predict="
  +format.format(predict)+"("+actualDirection+")"
  +",diff="+diff);
}
```

Finally, display stats on the overall accuracy of the neural network.

```
double percent = (double)correct/(double)count;
System.out.println("Direction correct:" + correct + "/" + count);
System.out.println("Directional Accuracy:"+format.format(percent
  *100)+"%");
}
```

The following code snippet shows the output of this application when launched once. Because it uses data preceding the current date, the results will be different when run. These results occur because the program is attempting to predict percent movement on Apple Computer's stock price.

Day 1: actual=0.05(up), predict=−0.09(up), diff=0.1331431391626865
Day 2: actual=−0.02(down), predict=0.15(down), diff =0.1752316137707985
Day 3: actual=−0.04(down), predict=−0.08(down), diff =0.04318588896364293
Day 4: actual=0.04(up), predict=−0.13(up), diff=0.167230163960771
Day 5: actual=0.04(up), predict=0.08(up), diff=0.041364210497886064
Day 6: actual=−0.05(down), predict=−0.15(down), diff =0.09856291235302134
Day 7: actual=0.03(up), predict=0.02(up), diff=0.0121349208067498
Day 8: actual=0.06(up), predict=0.14(up), diff=0.07873950162422072
Day 9: actual=0.00(up), predict=−0.04(up), diff=0.044884229765456175
Day 10: actual=−0.02(down), predict=−0.11(down), diff =0.08800357702537594
Day 11: actual=−0.03(down), predict=0.10(down), diff =0.1304932331559785
Day 12: actual=0.03(up), predict=−0.00(up), diff=0.03830226924277358
Day 13: actual=−0.04(down), predict=−0.03(down), diff =0.006017023124087514
Day 14: actual=0.01(up), predict=−0.00(up), diff=0.011094798099546017
Day 15: actual=−0.07(down), predict=0.10(down), diff =0.1634993352860712
Day 16: actual=0.00(up), predict=0.09(up), diff=0.08529079398874763
Day 17: actual=0.01(up), predict=0.08(up), diff=0.07476901867409716
Day 18: actual=−0.05(down), predict=0.10(down), diff =0.14462998342498684
Day 19: actual=0.01(up), predict=0.01(up), diff=0.0053944458622837204
Day 20: actual=−0.02(down), predict=0.16(down), diff =0.17692298105888082
Day 21: actual=0.01(up), predict=0.01(up), diff=0.003908063600862748
Day 22: actual=0.01(up), predict=0.05(up), diff=0.04043842368088156
Day 23: actual=−0.00(down), predict=0.05(down), diff =0.05856519756505361
Day 24: actual=−0.01(down), predict=−0.01(down), diff =0.0031913517175624975
Day 25: actual=0.06(up), predict=0.03(up), diff=0.02967685979492382
Day 26: actual=0.04(up), predict=−0.01(up), diff=0.05155871532643232
Day 27: actual=−0.02(down), predict=−0.09(down), diff =0.06931714317358993
Day 28: actual=−0.02(down), predict=−0.04(down), diff =0.019323500655091908
Day 29: actual=0.02(up), predict=0.06(up), diff=0.04364949212592098

```
Day 30: actual = −0.02(down), predict = −0.06(down), diff
    = 0.036886336426948246
Direction correct:18/30
Directional Accuracy:60.00%
```

Here, the program had an accuracy of 60%, which is very good for this simple neural network. Accuracy rates generally range from 30-40% when this program was run at different intervals.

This is a very simple stock market predictor and should not be used for any actual investing. It shows how to structure a neural network to predict market direction.

8.6   Summary

In this chapter, we learned how Encog could process temporal neural networks. Temporal networks are used to predict what will occur in the future. The first example in this chapter showed how to use Encog to predict sunspots. The second example showed how to use Encog to attempt to predict stock price movements.

The sunspot example made use of the **TemporalDataSet**. This is a low-level temporal dataset that is designed to model any "window-based" prediction neural network. A past window is used to provide several values to the neural network from which to make predictions. A future window specifies the number of elements the neural network should predict into the future.

The stock market example used the **MarketMLDataSet** class. This class is based on the **TemporalDataSet** to automatically download financial information from Yahoo Finance. This is a very simple example to show the foundation of applying neural networks to the stock market. Investment decisions should not be made based on this network.

The next chapter will show how to use images with neural networks. Presenting images to a neural network is a matter of converting the image into a numeric array so that a neural network will consider it as input. This is true for any information to be presented to a neural network. It is a matter of converting that data into an array of floating point values.

Chapter 9

Using Image Data

- Processing Images

- Finding the Bounds

- Downsampling

- Using the Image Dataset

Using neural networks to recognize images is a very common task. This chapter will explore how to use images with Encog. By using the same feedforward neural networks as seen in earlier chapters, neural networks can be designed to recognize certain images. Specialized datasets ease the process of getting image data into the neural network.

This chapter will introduce the **ImageMLDataSet**. This class can accept a list of images that will be loaded and processed into an Encog-friendly form. The **ImageMLDataSet** is based upon the **BasicMLDataSet**, which is really just an array of double values for input and idea. The **ImageMLDataSet** simply adds special functions to load images into arrays of doubles.

There are several important issues to consider when loading image data into a neural network. The **ImageMLDataSet** takes care of two important aspects of this. The first aspect is detecting boundaries on what is to be recognized. The second is downsampling where images are usually formatted in high-resolution and must be downsampled to a consistent lower resolution to be fed to the neural network.

9.1   Finding the Bounds

An image is a rectangular region that represents the data important to the neural network. Only a part of the image may be useful. Ideally, the actual image the neural network must recognize is equal to the entire physical image - rather than just a portion of the original image. Such is the case with Figure 9.1.

Figure 9.1: An X Drawn Over the Entire Drawing Area

As you can see in the above figure, the letter "X" was drawn over nearly the entire physical image. This image would require minimal, if any, boundary detection.

Images will not always be so perfectly created. Consider the image presented in Figure 9.2.

Figure 9.2: An Off-Center, Off-Scale X

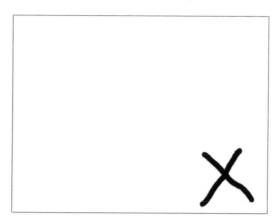

Here the letter "X" is scaled differently than in the previous image and is also off-center. To properly recognize it, we must find the bounds of the second letter "X." Figure 9.3 shows a bounding box around the letter "X." Only data inside of the bounding box will be used to recognize the image.

Figure 9.3: The X with its Bounds Detected

As you can see, the bounds have been detected for the letter "X." The bounding box signifies that only data inside of that box will be recognized. Now the "X" is in approximately the same orientation as Figure 9.1.

9.2   Downsampling an Image

Even with bounding boxes, images may not be consistently sized. The letter
"X" in Figure 9.3 is considerably smaller than Figure 9.1. When recognizing
the image, we will draw a grid over the image and line up each grid cell to
an input neuron. To do this, the images must be consistently sized. Further,
most images have too high a resolution to be used with a neural network.

Downsampling solves both of these problems by reducing the image resolution and scaling all images to a consistent size. To see this in action, consider
Figure 9.4. This figure shows the Encog logo at full resolution.

Figure 9.4: The Encog Logo at Full Resolution

Figure 9.5 shows this same image downsampled.

Figure 9.5: The Encog Logo Downsampled

Do you notice the grid-like pattern? It has been reduced to 32x32 pixels.
These pixels would form the input to a neural network. This neural network
would require 1,024 input neurons, if the network were to only look at the
intensity of each square. Looking at the intensity limits the neural network to
see in "black and white."

If you would like the neural network to seen in color, then it is necessary to provide red, green and blue (RGB) values for each of these pixels. This would mean three input neurons for each pixel, which would push the input neuron count to 3,072.

The Encog image dataset provides both boundary detection, as well as RGB and intensity downsampling. In the next section, the Encog image dataset will be introduced.

9.2.1   What to Do With the Output Neurons

The output neurons should represent the groups that these images will fall into. For example, if writing an OCR application, use one output neuron for every character to be recognized. Equilateral encoding is also useful in this respect, as discussed in Chapter 2 "Obtaining Data for Encog."

Supervised training also requires ideal output data for each image. For a simple OCR, there might be 26 output neurons, one for each letter of the alphabet. These ideal outputs train the neural network for what the image actually is. Whether training is supervised or unsupervised training, the output neurons will relay how the neural network interpreted each image.

9.3   Using the Encog Image Dataset

Before instantiating an **ImageMLDataSet** object, a downsampled object must be created. This object is a tool for Encog to use to perform the downsample. All Encog downsample objects must implement the interface **Downsample**. Encog currently supports two downsample classes, listed below:

- **RGBDownsample**

- **SimpleIntensityDownsample**

The **SimpleIntensityDownsample** does not take color into consideration. It simply calculates the brightness or darkness of a pixel. The number of input neurons will be height multiplied by the width, as there is only one input neuron needed per pixel.

The **RGBDownsample** is more advanced than **SimpleIntensityDown-sample**. This downsample object converts to the resolution that you specify and turns every pixel into a three-color (RGB) input. The total number of input neuron values produced by this object will be height times width times three. The following code instantiates a **SimpleIntensityDownsample** object. This object will be used to create the training set.

```
downsample = new SimpleIntensityDownsample();
```

Now that a downsample object is created, it is time to use an **ImageML-DataSet** class. It must be instantiated with several parameters. The following code does this.

```
training = new ImageMLDataSet( downsample, false, 1, -1);
```

The parameters 1 and -1 specify the range to which the colors will be normalized, either by the intensity color or the three individual RGB colors. The **false** value means that the dataset should not attempt to detect the edges. If this value were **true**, Encog would attempt to detect the edges.

The current Encog edge detection is not very advanced. It looks for one consistent color around the sides of an image and attempts to remove as much of that region as it can. More advanced edge detection will likely be built into future versions of Encog. If advanced edge detection is necessary, it is best to trim the images before sending them to the **ImageMLDataSet** object.

Now that the **ImageMLDataSet** object has been created, it is time to add some images. To add images to this dataset, an **ImageMLData** object must be created for each image. The following lines of code will add one image from a file.

```
Image img = ImageIO.read( [filename of image] );
ImageMLData data = new ImageMLData( img );
this.training.add( data, [ideal output] );
```

The image is loaded from a file using the Java **ImageIO** class, which reads images from files. Any valid Java image object can be used by the dataset.

The ideal output should be specified when using supervised training. With unsupervised training, this parameter can be omitted. Once the **ImageML-Data** object is instantiated, it is added to the dataset. These steps are repeated for every image to be added.

Once all of the images are loaded, they are ready to be downsampled. To downsample the images call the **downsample** method.

```
this.training.downsample( [downsample height] ,
   [downsample width] );
```

Specify the downsample height and width. All of the images will be downsampled to this size. After calling the **downsample** method, the training data is generated and can train a neural network.

9.4   Image Recognition Example

We will now see how to tie all Encog image classes together into an example. A generic image recognition program will serve as an example and could easily become the foundation of a much more complex image recognition program. This example is driven from a script file. Listing 9.1 shows the type of script file that might drive this program.

Listing 9.1: Image Recognition Script

```
CreateTraining:  width:16,height:16,type:RGB
Input:  image:./coins/dime.png, identity:dime
Input:  image:./coins/dollar.png, identity:dollar
Input:  image:./coins/half.png, identity:half dollar
Input:  image:./coins/nickle.png, identity:nickle
Input:  image:./coins/penny.png, identity:penny
Input:  image:./coins/quarter.png, identity:quarter
Network:  hidden1:100, hidden2:0
Train:  Mode:console , Minutes:1, StrategyError:0.25 , StrategyCycles
   :50
Whatis:  image:./coins/dime.png
Whatis:  image:./coins/half.png
Whatis:  image:./coins/testcoin.png
```

The syntax used by this script file is very simple. There is a command, followed by a colon. This command is followed by a comma-separated list of parameters. Each parameter is a name-value pair that is also separated by a colon. There are five commands in all: **CreateTraining**, **Input**, **Network**, **Train** and **WhatIs**.

The **CreateTraining** command creates a new training set. To do so, specify the downsample height, width, and type - either RGB or Brightness.

The **Input** command inputs a new image for training. Each input command specifies the image as well as the identity of the image. Multiple images can have the same identity. For example, the above script could have provided a second image of a dime by causing the second **Input** command to also have the identity of "dime."

The **Network** command creates a new neural network for training and recognition. Two parameters specify the size of the first and second hidden layers. If you do not wish to have a second hidden layer, specify zero for the **hidden2** parameter.

The **Train** command trains the neural network and mode specifies either console or GUI training. The **minutes** parameter specifies how many minutes are required to train the network. This parameter is only used with console training; for GUI training this parameter should be set to zero. The strategy tells the training algorithm how many cycles to wait to reset the neural network if the error level has not dropped below the specified amount.

The **WhatIs** command accepts an image and tries to recognize it. The example will print the identity of the image that it thought was most similar.

We will now take a look at the image recognition example. This example can be found at the following location.

```
org.encog.examples.neural.image.ImageNeuralNetwork
```

Some of the code in the above example deals with parsing the script file and arguments. Because string parsing is not really the focus of this book, we will focus on how each command is carried out and how the neural network is constructed. The next sections discuss how each of these commands is implemented.

9.4.1   Creating the Training Set

The **CreateTraining** command is implemented by the **processCreateTraining** method. This method is shown here.

```
private void processCreateTraining() {
```

The **CreateTraining** command takes three parameters. The following lines read these parameters.

```
final String strWidth = getArg("width");
final String strHeight = getArg("height");
final String strType = getArg("type");
```

The **width** and **height** parameters are both integers and need to be parsed.

```
this.downsampleHeight = Integer.parseInt(strWidth);
this.downsampleWidth = Integer.parseInt(strHeight);
```

We must now create the downsample object. If the mode is RGB, use **RGB-Downsample**. Otherwise, use **SimpleIntensityDownsample**.

```
if (strType.equals("RGB")) {
    this.downsample = new RGBDownsample();
} else {
    this.downsample = new SimpleIntensityDownsample();
}
```

The **ImageMLDataSet** can now be created.

```
this.training = new ImageMLDataSet(
    this.downsample, false, 1, -1);
System.out.println("Training set created");
}
```

Now that the training set is created, we can input images. The next section describes how this is done.

9.4.2 Inputting an Image

The **Input** command is implemented by the **processInput** method. This method is shown here.

```
private void processInput() throws IOException {
```

The **Input** command takes two parameters. The following lines read these parameters.

```
final String image = getArg("image");
final String identity = getArg("identity");
```

The identity is a text string that represents what the image is. We track the number of unique identities and assign an increasing number to each. These unique identities will form the neural network's output layer. Each unique identity will be assigned an output neuron. When images are presented to the neural network later, the output neuron with the highest output will represent the image identity to the network. The **assignIdentity** method is a simple method that assigns this increasing count and maps the identity strings to their neuron index.

```
final int idx = assignIdentity(identity);
```

A **File** object is created to hold the image. This will later be used to also read the image.

```
final File file = new File(image);
```

At this point we do not wish to actually load the individual images. We will simply make note of the image by saving an **ImagePair** object. The **ImagePair** object links the image to its output neuron index number. The **ImagePair** class is not built into Encog. Rather, it is a structure used by this example to map the images.

```
this.imageList.add(new ImagePair(file, idx));
```

Finally, we display a message that tells us that the image has been added.

```
System.out.println("Added input image:" + image);
}
```

Once all the images are added, the number of output neurons is apparent and we can create the actual neural network. Creating the neural network is explained in the next section.

9.4.3 Creating the Network

The **Network** command is implemented by the **processInput** method. This method is shown here.

```
private void processNetwork() throws IOException {
```

Begin by downsampling the images. Loop over every **ImagePair** previously created.

```
System.out.println("Downsampling images...");
for (final ImagePair pair : this.imageList) {
```

Create a new **BasicMLData** to hold the ideal output for each output neuron.

```
final MLData ideal = new
    BasicMLData(this.outputCount);
```

The output neuron that corresponds to the identity of the image currently being trained will be set to 1. All other output neurons will be set to -1.

```
final int idx = pair.getIdentity();
for (int i = 0; i < this.outputCount; i++) {
if (i == idx) {
   ideal.setData(i, 1);
}
else {
   ideal.setData(i, -1);     }
}
```

The input data for this training set item will be the downsampled image. First, load the image into a Java **Image** object.

```
final Image img = ImageIO.read(pair.getFile());
```

Create an **ImageMLData** object to hold this image and add it to the training set.

```
final ImageMLData data = new ImageMLData(img);
this.training.add(data, ideal);
}
```

There are two parameters provided to the **Network** command that specify the number of neurons in each of the two hidden layers. If the second hidden layer has no neurons, there is a single hidden layer.

```
final String strHidden1 = getArg("hidden1");
final String strHidden2 = getArg("hidden2");
final int hidden1 = Integer.parseInt(strHidden1);
final int hidden2 = Integer.parseInt(strHidden2);
```

We are now ready to downsample all of the images.

```
this.training.downsample(
    this.downsampleHeight, this.downsampleWidth);
```

Finally, the new neural network is created according to the specified parameters. The final **true** parameter specifies that we would like to use a hyperbolic tangent activation function.

```
this.network = EncogUtility.simpleFeedForward(
    this.training.getInputSize(),
    hidden1, hidden2,
    this.training.getIdealSize(), true);
```

Once the network is created, report its completion by printing a message.

```
System.out.println("Created network: " +
    this.network.toString());
}
```

Now that the network has been created, it can be trained. Training is handled in the next section.

9.4.4 Training the Network

The **Train** command is implemented by the **processTrain** method. This method is shown here.

```
private void processTrain() throws IOException {
```

The **Train** command takes four parameters. The following lines read these parameters.

```
final String strMode = getArg("mode");
final String strMinutes = getArg("minutes");
final String strStrategyError = getArg("strategyerror");
final String strStrategyCycles = getArg("strategycycles");
```

Once the parameters are read, display a message stating that training has begun.

```
System.out.println("Training Beginning... Output patterns="
  + this.outputCount);
```

Parse the two strategy parameters.

```
final double strategyError = Double.parseDouble(strStrategyError
    );
final int strategyCycles = Integer.parseInt(strStrategyCycles);
```

The neural network is initialized to random weight and threshold values. Sometimes the random set of weights and thresholds will cause the neural network training to stagnate. In this situation, reset a new set of random values and begin training again.

Training is initiated by creating a new **ResilientPropagation** trainer. RPROP training was covered in Chapter 5 "Propagation Training."

```
final ResilientPropagation train =
  new ResilientPropagation(this.network, this.training);
```

Encog allows training strategies to be added to handle situations such as this. One particularly useful training strategy is the **ResetStrategy**, which takes two parameters. The first states the minimum error that the network must achieve before it will be automatically reset to new random values. The second parameter specifies the number of cycles that the network is allowed to achieve this error rate. If the specified number of cycles is reached and the network is not at the required error rate, the weights and thresholds will be randomized.

Encog supports a number of different training strategies. Training strategies enhance whatever training method in use. They allow minor adjustments as training progresses. Encog supports the following strategies:

- **Greedy**

- **HybridStrategy**

- **ResetStrategy**

- **SmartLearningRate**

- **SmartMomentum**

- **StopTrainingStrategy**

The **Greedy** strategy only allows a training iteration to save its weight and threshold changes if the error rate was improved. The **HybridStrategy** allows a backup training method to be used if the primary training method stagnates. The hybrid strategy was explained in Chapter 7 "Other Neural Network Types." The **ResetStrategy** resets the network if it stagnates. The **SmartLearningRate** and **SmartMomentum** strategies are used with back-propagation training to attempt to automatically adjust momentum and learning rate. The **StopTrainingStrategy** stops training if it has reached a certain level.

The following lines of code add a reset strategy.

```
train.addStrategy(
    new ResetStrategy(strategyError, strategyCycles));
```

If we are truing using the GUI, then we must use **trainDialog**, otherwise we should use **trainConsole**.

```
if (strMode.equalsIgnoreCase("gui")) {
    EncogUtility.trainDialog(train, this.network, this.training);
} else {
    final int minutes = Integer.parseInt(strMinutes);
    EncogUtility.trainConsole(train, this.network, this.training,
        minutes);
}
```

The program will indicate that training has stopped by displaying a message such as the one shown below. The training process stops when it is canceled by the dialog or, in the case of GUI mode, has been canceled.

```
System.out.println("Training Stopped...");
}
```

Once the neural network is trained, it is ready to recognize images. This is discussed in the next section.

9.4.5   Recognizing Images

The **WhatIs** command is implemented by the **processWhatIs** method. This method is shown here.

```
public void processWhatIs() throws IOException {
```

The **WhatIs** command takes one parameter. The following lines read this parameter.

```
final String filename = getArg("image");
```

The image is then loaded into an ImageMLData object.

```
final File file = new File(filename);
final Image img = ImageIO.read(file);
final ImageMLData input = new ImageMLData(img);
```

The image is downsampled to the correct dimensions.

```
input.downsample(this.downsample, false, this.downsampleHeight,
    this.downsampleWidth, 1, -1);
```

The downsampled image is presented to the neural network, which chooses the "winner" neuron. The winning neuron is the neuron with the greatest output for the pattern that was presented. This is simple "one-of" normalization as discussed in Chapter 2. Chapter 2 also introduced equilateral normalization, which could also be used.

```
final int winner = this.network.winner(input);
System.out.println("What is: " + filename + ", it seems to be: "
    + this.neuron2identity.get(winner));
}
```

Finally, we display the pattern recognized by the neural network.

This example demonstrated a simple script-based image recognition program. This application could easily be used as the starting point for other more advanced image recognition applications. One very useful extension to this application may be the ability to load and save the trained neural network.

9.5   Summary

This chapter demonstrated how to use images as input into Encog. Nearly any of the neural network types discussed in this book can be used to recognize images. The classes provided by Encog primarily process the image data into a form that is usable for a neural network, rather than defining the actual structure of the neural network.

The classes provided by Encog for image handling provide several very important functions including bounds detection and downsampling.

Bounds detection is the process that trims unimportant parts of an image. Encog supports simple bounds checking where a background of a consistent color can be removed. This prevents an object within the input image from impairing the neural network's ability to recognize the image. If bounds detection is used, it should not matter if the image to recognize is in the upper left or bottom right corner.

Downsampling is the process where the resolution of an image is decreased. Images can be very high-resolution and often consist of a large amount of color. Encog provides downsampling to deal with both issues. Images can be decreased to a much lower resolution so to reduce the number of input neurons. Downsampling can also discard color information and deal only with intensity.

In this book we have looked at a number of different neural network types. This chapter showed how feedforward neural networks can be applied to images. The self-organizing map (SOM) is another neural network type frequently used with images. The next chapter will look at the SOM.

Chapter 10

Using a Self-Organizing Map

- What is a self-organizing map (SOM)?

- Mapping colors with a SOM

- Training a SOM

- Applying the SOM to the forest cover data

This chapter focuses on using Encog to implement a self-organizing map (SOM). A SOM is a special type of neural network that classifies data. Typically, a SOM will map higher resolution data to a single or multidimensional output. This can help a neural network see the similarities among its input data. Dr. Teuvo Kohonen of the Academy of Finland created the SOM. Because of this, the SOM is sometimes called a Kohonen neural network.

Encog provides two different means by which SOM networks can be trained:

- Neighborhood Competitive Training

- Cluster Copy

Both training types are unsupervised. This means that no ideal data is provided. The network is simply given the data and the number of categories that data should be clustered into. During training, the SOM will cluster all of the training data. Additionally, the SOM will be capable of clustering new data without retraining.

The neighborhood competitive training method implements the classic SOM training model. The SOM is trained using a competitive, unsupervised training algorithm. Encog implements this training algorithm using the **BasicTrainSOM** class. This is a completely different type of training then those previously used in this book. The SOM does not use a training set or scoring object. There are no clearly defined objectives provided to the neural network at all. The only type of "objective" that the SOM has is to group similar inputs together.

The second training type provided by Encog is a cluster copy. This is a very simple training method that simply sets the weights into a pattern to accelerate the neighborhood competitive training. This training method can also be useful with a small training set where the number of training set elements exactly matches the number of clusters. The cluster copy training method is implemented in the **SOMClusterCopyTraining** class.

The first example in this chapter will take colors as input and map similar colors together. This GUI example program will visually show how similar colors are grouped together by the self-organizing map.

The output from a self-organizing map is topological. This output is usually viewed in an n-dimensional way. Often, the output is single dimensional, but it can also be two-dimensional, three-dimensional, even four-dimensional or higher. This means that the "position" of the output neurons is important. If two output neurons are closer to each other, they will be trained together more so than two neurons that are not as close.

All of the neural networks that examined so far in this book have not been topological. In previous examples from this book, the distance between neurons was unimportant. Output neuron number two was just as significant to output neuron number one as was output neuron number 100.

10.1   The Structure and Training of a SOM

An Encog SOM is implemented as a two-layer neural network. The SOM simply has an input layer and an output layer. The input layer maps data to the output layer. As patterns are presented to the input layer, the output neuron with the weights most similar to the input is considered the winner. This similarity is calculated by comparing the Euclidean distance between eight sets of weights and the input neurons. The shortest Euclidean distance wins. Euclidean distance calculation is covered in the next section.

There are no bias values in the SOM as in the feedforward neural network. Rather, there are only weights from the input layer to the output layer. Additionally, only a linear activation function is used.

10.1.1   Structuring a SOM

We will study how to structure a SOM. This SOM will be given several colors to train on. These colors will be expressed as RGB vectors. The individual red, green and blue values can range between -1 and +1. Where -1 is no color, or black, and +1 is full intensity of red, green or blue. These three-color components comprise the neural network input.

The output is a 2,500-neuron grid arranged into 50 rows by 50 columns. This SOM will organize similar colors near each other in this output grid. Figure 10.1 shows this output.

Figure 10.1: The Output Grid

The above figure may not be as clear in black and white editions of this book as it is in color. However, you can see similar colors grouped near each other. A single, color-based SOM is a very simple example that allows you to visualize the grouping capabilities of the SOM.

10.1.2   Training a SOM

How is a SOM trained? The training process will update the weight matrix, which is 3 x2,500. Initialize the weight matrix to random values to start. Then 15 training colors are randomly chosen.

Just like previous examples, training will progress through a series of iterations. However, unlike feedforward neural networks, SOM networks are usually trained with a fixed number of iterations. For the colors example in this chapter, we will use 1,000 iterations.

Begin training the color sample that we wish to train for by choosing one random color sample per iteration. Pick one output neuron whose weights most closely match the basis training color. The training pattern is a vector of three numbers. The weights between each of the 2,500 output neurons and the three input neurons are also a vector of three numbers. Calculate the Euclidean distance between the weight and training pattern. Both are a vector of three numbers. This is done with Equation 10.1.

$$d(\mathbf{p}, \mathbf{w}) = \sqrt{\sum_{i=1}^{n} (p_i - w_i)^2} \tag{10.1}$$

This is very similar to Equation 2.3, shown in Chapter 2. In the above equation the variable $\mathbf{p}$ represents the input pattern. The variable $\mathbf{w}$ represents the weight vector. By squaring the differences between each vector component and taking the square root of the resulting sum, we realize the Euclidean distance. This measures how different each weight vector is from the input training pattern.

This distance is calculated for every output neuron. The output neuron with the shortest distance is called the Best Matching Unit (BMU). The BMU is the neuron that will learn the most from the training pattern. The neighbors of the BMU will learn less. Now that a BMU is determined, loop over all weights in the matrix. Update every weight according to Equation 10.2.

$$W_v(t + 1) = W_v(t) + \theta(v, t)\alpha(t)(D(t) - W_v(t)) \tag{10.2}$$

In the above equation, the variable $\mathbf{t}$ represents time, or the iteration number. The purpose of the equation is to calculate the resulting weight vector $\mathbf{Wv(t+1)}$. The next weight will be calculated by adding to the current weight, which is $\mathbf{Wv(t)}$. The end goal is to calculate how different the current weight is from the input vector. The clause $\mathbf{D(T)}$-$\mathbf{Wv(t)}$ achieves this. If we simply added this value to the weight, the weight would exactly match the input vector. We don't want to do this. As a result, we scale it by multiplying it by two ratios. The first ratio, represented by theta, is the neighborhood function. The second ratio is a monotonically decreasing learning rate.

The neighborhood function considers how close the output neuron we are training is to the BMU. For closer neurons, the neighborhood function will be close to one. For distant neighbors the neighborhood function will return zero. This controls how near and far neighbors are trained. We will look at how the neighborhood function determines this in the next section.

The learning rate also scales how much the output neuron will learn. This learning rate is similar to the learning rate used in backpropagation training. However, the learning rate should decrease as the training progresses. This learning rate must decrease monotonically, meaning the function output only decreases or remains the same as time progresses. The output from the function will never increase at any interval as time increases.

10.1.3 Understanding Neighborhood Functions

The neighborhood function determines to what degree each output neuron should receive training from the current training pattern. The neighborhood function will return a value of one for the BMU. This indicates that it should receive the most training of any neurons. Neurons further from the BMU will receive less training. The neighborhood function determines this percent.

If the output is arranged in only one dimension, a simple one-dimensional neighborhood function should be used. A single dimension self-organizing map treats the output as one long array of numbers. For instance, a single dimension network might have 100 output neurons that are simply treated as a long, single dimension array of 100 values.

A two-dimensional SOM might take these same 100 values and treat them as a grid, perhaps of 10 rows and 10 columns. The actual structure remains the same; the neural network has 100 output neurons. The only difference is the neighborhood function. The first would use a single dimensional neighborhood function; the second would use a two-dimensional neighborhood function. The function must consider this additional dimension and factor it into the distance returned.

It is also possible to have three, four, and even more dimensional functions for the neighborhood function. Two-dimension is the most popular choice. Single dimensional neighborhood functions are also somewhat common. Three or more dimensions are more unusual. It really comes down to computing how many ways an output neuron can be close to another. Encog supports any number of dimensions, though each additional dimension adds greatly to the amount of memory and processing power needed.

The Gaussian function is a popular choice for a neighborhood function.

The Gaussian function has single- and multi-dimensional forms. The single-dimension Gaussian function is shown in Equation 10.3.

$$f(x) = ae^{-\frac{(x-b)^2}{2c^2}}$$ (10.3)

The graph of the Gaussian function is shown in Figure 10.2.

Figure 10.2: A One-Dimensional Gaussian Function

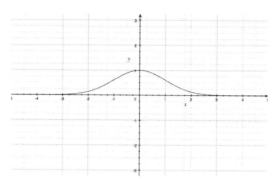

The above figure shows why the Gaussian function is a popular choice for a neighborhood function. If the current output neuron is the BMU, then its distance (x-axis) will be zero. As a result, the training percent (y-axis) is 100%. As the distance increases either positively or negatively, the training percentage decreases. Once the distance is great enough, the training percent is near zero.

There are several constants in Equation 10.3 that govern the shape of the Gaussian function. The constants **a** is the height of the curve's peak, **b** is the position of the center of the peak, and **c** constants the width of the "bell". The variable x represents the distance that the current neuron is from the BMU.

The above Gaussian function is only useful for a one-dimensional output array. If using a two-dimensional output grid, it is important to use the two-dimensional form of the Gaussian function. Equation 10.4 shows this.

$$f(x, y) = Ae^{-\left(\frac{(x-x_o)^2}{2\sigma_x^2} + \frac{(y-y_o)^2}{2\sigma_y^2}\right)}$$ (10.4)

The graph form of the two-dimensional form of the Gaussian function is shown in Figure 10.3.

Figure 10.3: A Two-Dimensional Gaussian Function

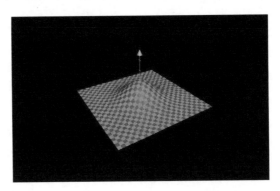

The two-dimensional form of the Gaussian function takes a single peak variable, but allows the user to specify separate values for the position and width of the curve. The equation does not need to be symmetrical.

How are the Gaussian constants used with a neural network? The peak is almost always one. To unilaterally decrease the effectiveness of training, the peak should be set below one. However, this is more the role of the learning rate. The center is almost always zero to center the curve on the origin. If the center is changed, then a neuron other than the BMU would receive the full learning. It is unlikely you would ever want to do this. For a multi-dimensional Gaussian, set all centers to zero to truly center the curve at the origin.

This leaves the width of the Gaussian function. The width should be set to something slightly less than the entire width of the grid or array. Then the width should be gradually decreased. The width should be decreased monotonically just like the learning rate.

10.1.4   Forcing a Winner

An optional feature to Encog SOM competitive training is the ability to force a winner. By default, Encog does not force a winner. However, this feature can be enabled for SOM training. Forcing a winner will try to ensure that each output neuron is winning for at least one of the training samples. This can cause a more even distribution of winners. However, it can also skew the data as somewhat "engineers" the neural network. Because of this, it is disabled by default.

10.1.5 Calculating Error

In propagation training we could measure the success of our training by examining the neural network current error. In a SOM there is no direct error because there is no expected output. Yet, the Encog interface **Train** exposes an error property. This property does return an estimation of the SOM error.

The error is defined to be the "worst" or longest Euclidean distance of any BMUs. This value should be minimized as learning progresses. This gives a general approximation of how well the SOM has been trained.

10.2 Implementing the Colors SOM in Encog

We will now see how the color matching SOM is implemented. There are two classes that make up this example:

- **MapPanel**

- **SomColors**

The **MapPanel** class is used to display the weight matrix to the screen. The **SomColors** class extends the **JPanel** class and adds the **MapPanel** to itself for display. We will examine both classes, starting with the **MapPanel**.

10.2.1 Displaying the Weight Matrix

The **MapPanel** class draws the GUI display for the SOM as it progresses. This relatively simple class can be found at the following location.

```
org.encog.examples.neural.gui.som.MapPanel
```

The **convertColor** function is very important. It converts a double that contains a range of -1 to +1 into the 0 to 255 range that an RGB component requires. A neural network deals much better with -1 to +1 than 0 to 255. As a result, this normalization is needed.

```
private int convertColor(double d) {
  double result = 128*d;
  result+=128;
  result = Math.min(result, 255);
  result = Math.max(result, 0);
  return (int)result;
}
```

The number 128 is the midpoint between 0 and 255. We multiply the **result** by 128 to get it to the proper range and then add 128 to diverge from the midpoint. This ensures that the result is in the proper range.

Using the **convertColor** method the **paint** method can properly draw the state of the SOM. The output from this function will be a color map of all of the neural network weights. Each of the 2,500 output neurons is shown on a grid. Their color is determined by the weight between that output neuron and the three input neurons. These three weights are treated as RGB color components. The **convertColor** method is shown here.

```
public void paint(Graphics g)
{
```

Begin by looping through all 50 rows and columns.

```
for(int y = 0; y< HEIGHT; y++)  {
  for(int x = 0; x< WIDTH; x++)  {
```

While the output neurons are shown as a two-dimensional grid, they are all stored as a one-dimensional array. We must calculate the current one-dimensional index from the two-dimensional **x** and **y** values.

```
int index = (y*WIDTH)+x;
```

We obtain the three weight values from the matrix and use the **convertColor** method to convert these to RGB components.

```
int red = convertColor(weights.get(0, index));
int green = convertColor(weights.get(1, index));
int blue = convertColor(weights.get(2, index));
```

These three components are used to create a new **Color** object.

```
    g.setColor(new Color(red,green,blue));
```

A filled rectangle is displayed to display the neuron.

```
g.fillRect(x*CELL_SIZE, y*CELL_SIZE, CELL_SIZE, CELL_SIZE);
    }
  }
}
```

Once the loops complete, the entire weight matrix has been displayed to the screen.

10.2.2   Training the Color Matching SOM

The **SomColors** class acts as the main **JPanel** for the application. It also provides the neural network all of the training. This class can be found at the following location.

```
package org.encog.examples.neural.gui.som.SomColors
```

The **BasicTrainSOM** class must be set up so that the neural network will train. To do so, a neighborhood function is required. For this example, use the **NeighborhoodGaussian** neighborhood function. This neighborhood function can support a multi-dimensional Gaussian neighborhood function. The following line of code creates this neighborhood function.

```
this.gaussian = new NeighborhoodRBF(RBFEnum.Gaussian,MapPanel.
    WIDTH,
MapPanel.HEIGHT);
```

This constructor creates a two-dimensional Gaussian neighborhood function. The first two parameters specify the height and width of the grid.

There are other constructors that can create higher dimensional Gaussian functions. Additionally, there are other neighborhood functions provided by Encog. The most common is the **NeighborhoodRBF**. **NeighborhoodRBF** can use a Gaussian, or other radial basis functions.

Below is the complete list of neighborhood functions.

- **NeighborhoodBubble**

- **NeighborhoodRBF**

- **NeighborhoodRBF1D**

- **NeighborhoodSingle**

The **NeighborhoodBubble** only provides one-dimensional neighborhood functions. A radius is specified and anything within that radius receives full training. The **NeighborhoodSingle** functions as a single-dimensional neighborhood function and only allows the BMU to receive training.

The **NeighborhoodRBF** class supports several RBF functions. The "Mexican Hat" and "Gaussian" RBF's are common choices. However the Multiquadric and the Inverse Multiquadric are also available.

We must also create a **CompetitiveTraining** object to make use of the neighborhood function.

```
this.train = new BasicTrainSOM(this.network, 0.01, null, gaussian)
    ;
```

The first parameter specifies the network to train and the second parameter is the learning rate. Automatically decrease the learning rate from a maximum value to a minimum value, so the learning rate specified here is not important. The third parameter is the training set. Randomly feed colors to the neural network, thus eliminating the need for the training set. Finally, the fourth parameter is the newly created neighborhood function.

The SOM training is provided for this example by a background thread. This allows the training to progress while the user watches. The background thread is implemented in the **run** method, as shown here.

```
public void run() {
```

The **run** method begins by creating the 15 random colors to train the neural network. These random samples will be stored in the **samples** variable, which is a **List**.

```
List <MLData> samples = new ArrayList <MLData>();
```

The random colors are generated and have random numbers for the RGB components.

```
for(int i=0;i<15;i++) {
    MLData data = new BasicMLData(3);
    data.setData(0, RangeRandomizer.randomize(-1,1));
    data.setData(1, RangeRandomizer.randomize(-1,1));
    data.setData(2, RangeRandomizer.randomize(-1,1));
    samples.add(data);
}
```

The following line sets the parameters for the automatic decay of the learning rate and the radius.

```
this.train.setAutoDecay(1000, 0.8, 0.003, 30, 5);
```

We must provide the anticipated number of iterations. For this example, the quantity is 1,000. For SOM neural networks, it is necessary to know the number of iterations up front. This is different than propagation training that trained for either a specific amount of time or until below a specific error rate.

The parameters 0.8 and 0.003 are the beginning and ending learning rates. The error rate will be uniformly decreased from 0.8 to 0.003 over each iteration. It should reach close to 0.003 by the last iteration.

Likewise, the parameters 30 and 5 represent the beginning and ending radius. The radius will start at 30 and should be near 5 by the final iteration. If more than the planned 1,000 iterations are performed, the radius and learning rate will not fall below their minimums.

```
for(int i=0;i<1000;i++) {
```

For each competitive learning iteration, there are two choices. First, you can choose to simply provide an **MLDataSet** that contains the training data and call the **iteration** method **CompetitiveTraining**.

Next we choose a random color index and obtain that color.

```
int idx = (int)(Math.random()*samples.size());
MLData c = samples.get(idx);
```

The **trainPattern** method will train the neural network for this random color pattern. The BMU will be located and updated as described earlier in this chapter.

```
this.train.trainPattern(c);
```

Alternatively, the colors could have been loaded into an **MLDataSet** object and the **iteration** method could have been used. However, training the patterns one at a time and using a random pattern looks better when displayed on the screen.

Next, call the **autoDecay** method to decrease the learning rate and radius according to the parameters previously specified.

```
this.train.autoDecay();
```

The screen is repainted.

```
this.map.repaint();
```

Finally, we display information about the current iteration.

```
System.out.println("Iteration " + i + ","
    + this.train.toString());
    }
}
```

This process continues for 1,000 iterations. By the final iteration, the colors will be grouped.

10.3   Summary

Up to this point in the book, all neural networks have been trained using a supervised training algorithm. This chapter introduced unsupervised training. Unsupervised training provides no feedback to the neural network like the error rates previously examined.

A very common neural network type that can be used with unsupervised training is the self-organizing map (SOM), or Kohonen neural network. This neural network type has only an input and output layer. This is a competitive neural network; the neuron that has the highest output is considered the winning neuron.

A SOM trains by taking an input pattern and seeing which output neuron has the closest weight values to this input pattern. The closest matching neuron, called the best matching unit (BMU) is then trained. All neighboring neurons are also trained. The neighboring neurons are determined by the neighborhood function, as is the degree to which neighbors are trained. The most commonly used neighborhood functions are variants of the Gaussian function.

This concludes this book on Encog programming. Encog is an ever-evolving project. For more information on current Encog projects and additional articles about Encog, visit the following URL:

http://www.encog.org/

Encog is very much shaped by input from its users. We would love to hear about how you are using Encog and what new features may be beneficial as well. No software product, or book, is perfect. Bug reports are also very helpful as well. There is a forum at the above URL that can be used for the discussion of this book and Encog.

Appendix A

Installing and Using Encog

- Downloading Encog

- Running Examples

- Running the Workbench

This appendix shows how to install and use Encog. This consists of downloading Encog from the Encog Web site, installing and running the examples. This section also explains how to run the Encog Workbench.

As Encog uses Java, this appendix instructs under the assumption that Java JSE version 6 or later is already downloaded and installed on your computer. The latest version of Java can be downloaded from the following web site:

http://java.sun.com/

The examples in this book were tested with JSE 6 and 7. Java is a cross-platform programming language; as such, Encog can run on a variety of platforms. Encog has been used on Macintosh and Linux operating systems. However, this appendix is written toward the Windows operating system. The screen shots illustrate procedures on the Windows 7 operating. However, Encog should run well on Windows XP or later.

It is also possible to use Encog with an IDE. Encog was primarily developed using the Eclipse IDE. However, it should work well with other Java IDE's such as Netbeans or IntelliJ.

Useful Encog set up information may also be found at the following web address.

http://www.heatonresearch.com/wiki/Encog_Examples

A.1   Installing Encog

The latest verion of Encog is always available for download from the following URL:

http://www.heatonresearch.com/encog/

This page contains the download link for the latest version of Encog, as well as the following files:

- The Encog Core

- The Encog Examples

- The Encog Workbench

To successfully study this book, it is necessary to download the examples and the workbench. The workbench is distributed as a universal executable JAR and is accessed by simply double-clicking on Windows, Linux or Mac. This JAR file and a few information files comprise the Encog workbench release.

Encog includes both Ant and Maven files to assist with building the examples. An IDE may also be used. For information on using Encog with an IDE, refer to the tutorials on following page.

http://www.heatonresearch.com/wiki/Getting_Started

Apache Ant can be obtained from the following URL.

http://ant.apache.org/

Encog contains an API reference in the core download. This documentation is contained in the standard Javadoc format. Instructions for installing Ant can be found at the above website. If using Encog with an IDE, it is not necessary to install Ant. Once Ant is correctly installed, the **ant** command may be issued from a command prompt. Figure A.1 shows the expected output of the **ant** command.

Figure A.1: Ant Successfully Installed

The Encog Core, Encog Examples and Encog Workbench files can also be extracted into local directories. This appendix is written assuming these files are extracted into the following directories:

- c:\encog-java-core-3.0.0\

- c:\encog-java-examples-3.0.0\

- c:\encog-workbench-win-3.0.0\

Now that Encog and Ant are installed on your computer, you are ready to compile the core and examples. If you only want to use an IDE, skip to that section in this Appendix.

A.2   Compiling the Encog Core

Unless you would like to modify Encog itself, it is unlikely that you would need to compile the Encog core. Compiling the Encog core will recompile and rebuild the Encog core JAR file. It is very easy to recompile the Encog core using Ant. Open a command prompt and move to the following directory.

```
c:\encog-java-core-3.0.0\
```

From here, issue the following Ant command.

```
ant
```

This will rebuild the Encog core. If this command is successful, you should see output similar to the following:

```
C:\encog-java-core-3.0.0>ant
Buildfile: build.xml
init:
compile:
doc:
    [javadoc] Generating Javadoc
    [javadoc] Javadoc execution
    [javadoc] Loading source files for package org.encog...
    [javadoc] Loading source files for package org.encog.bot...
    [javadoc] Loading source files for package org.encog.bot.browse
        ...
    [javadoc] Loading source files for package org.encog.bot.browse.
        extract...
    [javadoc] Loading source files for package org.encog.bot.browse.
        range...
    [javadoc] Loading source files for package org.encog.bot.
        dataunit...
    [javadoc] Loading source files for package org.encog.bot.rss...
    [javadoc] Loading source files for package org.encog.matrix...
    [javadoc] Loading source files for package org.encog.neural...
    [javadoc] Loading source files for package org.encog.neural.
        activation...
    ...
    [javadoc] Loading source files for package org.encog.util.math
        ...
    [javadoc] Loading source files for package org.encog.util.math.
        rbf...
```

```
  [javadoc] Loading source files for package org.encog.util.
     randomize...
  [javadoc] Loading source files for package org.encog.util.time
     ...
  [javadoc] Constructing Javadoc information...
  [javadoc] Standard Doclet version 1.6.0_16
  [javadoc] Building tree for all the packages and classes...
  [javadoc] Building index for all the packages and classes...
  [javadoc] Building index for all classes...
dist:
BUILD SUCCESSFUL
Total time: 4 seconds
C:\encog-java-core-3.0.0>
```

This will result in a new Encog core JAR file being placed inside of the **lib** directory.

A.3 Compiling and Executing Encog Examples

The Encog examples are placed in a hierarchy of directories. The root example directory is located here.

```
c:\encog-java-examples-3.0.0\
```

The actual example JAR file is placed in a **lib** subdirectory off of the above directory. The examples archive already downloaded contains such a JAR file. It is not necessary to recompile the examples JAR file unless you make changes to one of the examples. To compile the examples, move to the root examples directory, given above.

A.3.1 Running an Example from the Command Line

When executing a Java application that uses Encog, the appropriate third-party JARs must be present in the Java **classpath**. The following command shows a way to execute the **XORHelloWorld** example:

```
java -cp ./lib/encog-core-3.0.0.jar;./lib/examples.jar org.encog.
    examples.neural.xor.XORHelloWorld
```

If the command does not work, make sure that the JAR files located in the **lib** and **jar** directories are present and named correctly. There may be new versions of these JAR files since this document was written. If this is the case, update the above command to match the correct JAR file names.

The Encog examples download for contains many examples. The Encog examples are each designed to be relatively short and are usually console applications. This makes them great starting points for creating your own application to use a neural network technology similar to the example. To run a different example, specify the package name and class name as was done above for **XORHelloWorld**.

You will also notice from the above example that the **-server** option was specified. This runs the application in Java server mode. Java server mode is very similar to the regular client mode. Programs run the same way, except server mode takes longer to start the program. But for this longer load time, you are rewarded with greater processing performance. Neural network applications are usually processing intense. As a result, it always pays to run them in server mode.

Glossary

Activation Function: A function used to scale the output of a neural network layer. If this activation function has a derivative, then propagation training can be used on the neural network.

Adaptive Resonance Theory (ART1): A neural network architecture that learns to classify patterns as they are presented.

Annealing Cycles: The number of cycles that the simulated annealing training method will use per iteration.

Artificial Intelligence (AI): A branch of computer science that seeks to give machines human-like intelligence. Neural networks are one tool used in AI.

Artificial Neural Network (ANN): See neural network.

Autoassociation: A means of pattern recognition where the output of the neural network is the entire pattern it recognized. The network returns the same data with which it was trained.

Backpropagation: A propagation algorithm where the error gradients are applied directly to the weight matrix, scaled only by a learning rate.

Backward Pass: One of two passes in propagation training where the error gradients are calculated and used to determine changes that should be made to the weight matrix of a neural network.

Basic Layer: A very versatile Encog neural network layer type that is used in many different neural networks. It has a number of neurons, an activation function and optional threshold values.

Batch Training: The accumulation of the weight matrix deltas from a number of training set elements before these deltas are actually applied to the weight matrix.

Best Matching Unit (BMU): The neuron, in a Self Organizing Map (SOM), that had the shortest Euclidean distance to the training data element. (BMU)

Bidirectional Associative Memory: A neural network type that forms bidirectional associations between two layers.

Biological Neural Network: The actual neural network contained in humans and other animals. This is what an artificial neural network attempts to simulate to some degree.

BiPolar: Activation Function: An activation function to support bipolar numbers. This maps a true value to 1 and a false value to -1.

Black Box: A computer system where the inputs and outputs are well understood; however, the means to produce the output is not known.

Boltzmann Machine: A simple recurrent neural network that adds a temperature element that randomizes the output of the neural network.

Bounding Box: A box that is drawn around the relevant part of an image.

Competitive Activation Function: An activation function where only a certain number of neurons are allowed to fire. These winning neurons were the ones with the highest activation.

Competitive Training: A training method, typically used by a Self Organizing Map, which chooses a best matching unit (BMU) and further strengthens that neuron's activation for the current training element.

Context Layer: An Encog layer type that remembers the input values from the last iteration and uses those values as the output for the current iteration. This layer type is used for simple, recurrent neural network types such as the Elman and Jordan neural networks.

Counter-Propagation Neural Network: A hybrid neural network that combines elements of a regular feedforward neural network and a Self Organizing Map. Counter-Propagation Neural Networks use both supervised and unsupervised training, which are called outstar and instar training respectively. (CPN)

Crop: The process where irrelevant portions of an image are removed.

Crossover: A simulation of the biological mating process in a Genetic Algorithm where elements from two "parent" solutions are combined to produce "offspring solutions" that share characteristics of both "parents".

CSV File: A comma separated value file. These are typically used as training input for an Encog neural network.

Derivative: In calculus, a measure of how a function changes as its input changes. Propagation training uses the derivative of the activation function to calculate an error gradient.

Direct Synapse: An Encog synapse that directly connects two layers of neurons. This layer type is typically used in a Radial Basis Function neural network.

Downsample: The process where the resolution and color depth of an image are reduced. This can make the image easier to recognize for a neural network.

EG File: An XML based file that Encog uses to store neural networks, training data and other objects.

Elman Neural Network: A simple recurrent neural network where the output of the hidden layer is fed to a context layer and then fed back into the hidden layer. The Elman Neural Network can be useful for temporal data.

Encog: An Artificial Intelligence Framework for Java, .Net and Silverlight that specializes in neural network applications.

Encog Benchmark: A means of calculating the performance of Encog on a particular machine. The benchmark is expressed as a number; a lower number indicates a faster machine. This benchmark uses multithreaded training and will score multicore machines higher.

Encog File: See EG file.

Encog Workbench: A GUI application that allows Encog EG files to be edited.

Ending Temperature: The temperature at which a simulated annealing iteration should end. The temperature defines the degree to which the weights are randomly perturbed in a simulated annealing cycle.

Epoch: See iteration.

Equilateral Normalization: A means by which nominal data is normalized for a neural network. Often provides better results than the competing one-of-n normalization.

Equilibrium: The point at which further iterations to a thermal neural network produce no further meaningful change.

Error Rate: The degree to which the output of neural network differs from the expected output.

Euclidian Distance: The square root of the squares of the individual differences in set of data. Euclidian Distance is often used to determine which vector is most similar to a comparison vector.

Evaluation: The process in which a trained neural network is evaluated against data that was not in the original training set.

Feedforward Neural Network: A multilayer neural network where connections only flow forward.

Field Group: A group of normalization output fields that depend on each other to calculate the output value.

Forward Pass: One of two passes in propagation training where the output from the neural network is calculated for a training element.

Future Window: The data that a temporal neural network is attempting to predict.

Gaussian Activation Function: An activation based on the Gaussian function.

Gaussian Neighborhood Function: A neighborhood function, used for a Self Organizing Map, based on the Gaussian function.

Genetic Algorithms: An Artificial Intelligence algorithm that attempts to derive a solution by simulating the biological process of natural selection.

Gradient Error: A value that is calculated for individual connections in the neural network that can provide insight into how the weight should be changed to lower the error of the neural network.

Greedy Training: A training strategy where iterations that do not lower the error rate of a neural network are discarded.

Hidden Layer: Layers in a neural network that exists between the input and output layers. They are used to assist the neural network in pattern recognition.

Hopfield Neural Network: A thermal neural network that contains a single self-connected layer.

Hybrid Training: Training a neural network with more than one training algorithm.

Hyperbolic Tangent Activation Function: An activation function that makes use of the hyperbolic tangent function. This activation function can return both positive and negative numbers.

Ideal Output: The expected output of a neural network.

Incremental Pruning: A means to automatically determine an efficient number of hidden neurons by increasing the hidden layer and testing each potential configuration.

Input Field: An Encog normalization field that accepts raw, un-normalized data. Input fields are provided that accept input from a number of different sources.

Input Layer: The layer in a neural network that accepts input.

Instar Training: An unsupervised training technique used for the counter-propagation neural network.

Intensity Downsample: A downsample technique where color information is discarded, and only the intensity, or brightness, of color is used.

Iteration: The basic unit of training where each iteration attempts to improve the neural network in some way.

Jordan Neural Network: A simple recurrent neural network where the output of the output layer is fed to a context layer and then fed back into the hidden layer. The Jordan Neural Network can be useful for temporal data.

Kohonen Neural Network: Another name for the Self Organizing Map (SOM).

Layer: A group of similar neurons in a neural network.

Layer Tag: The means by which Encog names layers.

Learning rate: The percentage of a change to the weight matrix that is allowed to occur. This allows changes that would overwhelm the neural network to be scaled to less dramatic values.

Lesser GNU Public License (LGPL): The license under which Encog is licensed.

Linear Activation Function: An activation function based on a simple linear function.

LOG Activation Function: An activation function based on logarithms.

Long Term Memory: The weights and threshold values of a neural network.

Lunar Lander Game: A classic computer game where the user fires thrusters to produce as soft a landing as possible, without running out of fuel.

Manhattan Update Rule: A propagation training technique where only the sign of the error gradient is used to determine the direction to change the connection weights. The magnitude of the error gradients is discarded.

Memory Collection: Encog persistence where the entire EG file is loaded into memory.

Momentum: The degree to which weight deltas from the pervious iteration are applied to the current iteration. Used in backpropagation to help avoid local minima.

Multicore: A computer capable of concurrently executing multiple threads. Software must be written to be multithreaded to use these machines to their full potential.

Multiplicative Normalization: A normalization technique to adjust a vector to sum to one. Multiplicative normalization has the effect of only using the magnitude of the input vector. To use sign and magnitude, z-axis normalization should be considered.

Multithreaded: A programming technique where the programming task is divided among multiple threads. This allows a multicore machine to greatly reduce the amount of time a program can take to execute.

Mutation: A technique used in Genetic Algorithms where the offspring are randomly changed in some way.

Neighborhood Function: A function that scales training in a Self Organizing Map to neurons near the best matching unit.

Network Pattern: A common neural network type, such as a Self Organizing Map, Elman network or Jordan network. Encog provides classes that assist in the creation of these neural network types.

Neural Logic: Encog classes that show Encog how to calculate the output for various types of neural networks.

Neural Network: A computerized simulation of an actual biological neural network. Sometimes referred to as an Artificial Neural Network (ANN); however, typically referred to as simply a "neural network".

Neural Network Properties: Operating parameters that certain neural network types require Encog to associate with the neural network.

Nominal Value: A value that is a member of a set, for example, male or female.

Normalization: The process where numbers are scaled in order to be acceptable input to a neural network.

Normalization Target: Where the Encog normalization classes are to store the results from the normalization value.

Numeric Value: A number value that is to be normalized that has meaning as a number. For example, altitude would be a numeric value, but a postal code would not.

One-to-One Synapse: An Encog synapse that directly connects each neuron in a layer to the corresponding neuron in another layer. A One-to-One Synapse is typically used to connect a basic layer to a context layer.

One-of-N Normalization: A means by which nominal data is normalized for a neural network. Often provides inferior results than the competing equilateral normalization.

Online Training: Training where the weight deltas are applied as soon as they are calculated.

Output Field: A normalization field that specified how an input field, or group of input fields, should be normalized.

Output Layer: The layer of a neural network that produces output.

Outstar Training: A supervised training technique used for the counter-propagation neural network.

Past Window: The values on which a temporal neural network bases future predictions.

Pattern: Data that is fed into a neural network.

Persistence: The ability to store data in a permanent form. Encog uses Encog EG files for persistence.

Plasticity: The ability of a neural network to change as data is fed to it.

Propagation Training: A group of training techniques that use error gradients to provide insight into how to update the weights of a neural network to achieve lower error rates. Forms of propagation training include backpropagation, resilient propagation, the Manhattan Update Rule, and others.

Pruning: Attempts to optimize the number of hidden neurons in a neural network.

Radial Basis Activation Function: An activation function based on a radial basis function.

Radial Basis Function (RBF): A function with its maximum value at its peak that decreases rapidly.

Radial Basis Function Layer: The layer, in a radial basis function network, that uses a compound radial basis function as its activation function.

Radial Basis Function Network: A special type of neural network that makes use of a radial basis function layer.

Recurrent Neural Network: A neural network that has connections back to previous layers.

Resilient Propagation (RPROP): A propagation training technique that uses independent delta values for every connection in the network. This is one of the most efficient training algorithms offered by Encog.

RGB: The red, green and blue values that make up an image.

RGB Downsample: A means of downsampling that preserves the color values of an image.

Scaling: See downsampling.

Score: A numeric value used to rank solutions provided by Genetic Algorithms and Simulated Annealing.

Segregator: An Encog normalization object that excludes certain elements, based on the criteria provided.

Selective Pruning: A pruning method where the weakest neurons are selected and removed.

Self-Organizing Map (SOM): A neural network structure that organizes similar input patterns.

Self-Connected Layer: A layer in a neural network that is connected to itself.

Serializable: A class that can be serialized.

Short Term Memory: A context layer provides neural network short-term memory.

Sigmoid Activation Function: An activation function based on the Sigmoid function. This activation function only produces positive values.

Simple Recurrent Neural Network (SRN): A neural network that has a recurrent connection through a context layer. The most typical SRN types are the Elman and Jordan neural networks.

Simulated Annealing: A training technique that simulates the metallurgical annealing process.

Sine Activation Function: An activation function based on the trigonometric sine function.

Single Threaded: An application that is not multithreaded. See multithreaded.

SoftMax Activation Function: An activation function that scales the output so the sum is one.

Staring Temperature: The temperature for the first simulated annealing cycle. (8)

Supervised Training: Training where the acceptability of the output of the neural network can be calculated.

Synapse: An Encog connection between two layers.

Temporal Data: Data that occurs over time.

Temporal Neural Network: A neural network that is designed to accept temporal data, and generally, offer a prediction.

Terminal Velocity: The maximum velocity that a falling object can obtain before friction brings acceleration to zero.

Thermal Neural Network: A neural network that contains a temperature; examples include the Hopfield Neural Network and the Boltzmann machine.

Threshold Value: Values kept on the layers of networks. Together with the weights, these are adjusted to train the network.

Training: The process of adjusting the weights and thresholds of a neural network to lower the error rate.

Training Set: Data that is used to train a neural network.

Traveling Salesman Problem: A computer problem where a traveling salesman must find the shortest route among a number of cities. (TSP)

Unsupervised Training: Training where no direction is given to the neural network as far as expected output.

Update Delta: The amount that training has determined a connection weight should be updated by.

Vector Length: The square root of the sum of the squares of a vector. This is a means of taking the average of the numbers in a vector.

Weight Matrix: The collection of connection weights between two layers.

Weighted Synapse: An Encog synapse between two layers that contains weights. This is the most common form of Encog synapse.

Weightless Synapse: A weight matrix that has no weights, only connections.

Window: A group of temporal data values.

XML File: A file that is encoded in XML; Encog saves objects to XML files.

XOR Operator: A logical operator that is only true when its two inputs do not agree.

Index

Made in the USA
Middletown, DE
11 November 2015